Cover: Private Collection

This issue is supported in part by:

NORTHWESTERN
UNIVERSITY
IN QATAR

ARABLIT QUARTERLY

VOLUME 4, ISSUE 3
Fall 2021

Editor-in-chief: M Lynx Qualey
Art Director: Hassân Al Mohtasib
Contributing Editors:
Nashwa Gowanlock, Sawad Hussain,
Olivia Snaije, Nariman Youssef,
Lucie Taylor, Joel Mitchell,
Ranya Abdel Rahman
Editorial Assistant:
Leonie Rau
Research Consultant:
Amanda Hannoosh Steinberg

A production of www.arablit.org
Opinions, submissions, advertising:
info@arablit.org
© All rights reserved

ك / و / ر

Kaf – Waw – Ra'

♦ **INTRODUCTION**

4   by M Lynx Qualey

♦ **FEATURES**

18 **Knocking on Freedom's Door**
    By Luqman Derky
    translated by Daniel Behar

28 **How Football Is Like Writing …**
    By Huda al-Daghfaq
    translated by Anam Zafar

50 **Farouk's Cosmos**
    By Khaled Ahmed Youssef
    translated by Becki Maddock

80 **Egyptian Football's Missing Archives**
    By Mina Ibrahim

92 **Football Games & Casual Gunfire**
    By Iraqi Shalash
    translated by Zeena Faulk

102 **Mahfouz's Armband**
    By Raja' al-Naqqash
    translated by Mahmoud Mostafa

112 **Matters of National Football**
    By Yassin Adnan
    translated by Hicham Rafik

♦ **POETRY**

26 **Fort-Da**
    By Hatem Alzahrani
    translated by Moneera Al-Ghadeer

40 **With a Hoarse Voice
    Football Chants from Five Countries**
    Edited by Leonie Rau

♦ **SHORT FICTION**

62 **The Roof**
    By Najwa Bin Shatwan
    translated by Nariman Youssef

64 **The Cloven Ball**
    By Yasmeen Hanoosh
    translated by Leonie Rau

68 **Captain Majid**
    By Ameer Hamad
    translated by M Lynx Qualey

70 **Captain Rabeh**
    By Ameer Hamad
    translated by M Lynx Qualey

72 **What If the Elephant
    Is the Room**
    By Muhammad El-Hajj
    translated by Yasmine Zohdi

76 **A Tin Ball**
    By Adania Shibli

100 **Diaries of a Running Man**
    Farid Abdel Azim
    translated by Omar Ibrahim

PAGE
80

Egyptian
Football's
Missing
Archives

كرة القدم
Introduction

By M Lynx Qualey

When Naguib Mahfouz was a boy, he tells us, two paths lay before him. There was the path of the literature he loved to read and write. He could take that path and become a distinguished author. There was also the path of the football he loved to play and the footballers he admired. He could take that, it was said, and become a member of the Egyptian Olympic football team.

Mahfouz, never one for half-measures, took the literary path and broke with football completely. As he says in the excerpt translated by Mahmoud Mostafa and published here, from Raja' al-Naqqash's *Naguib Mahfouz: Pages from his Memoirs and a New Perspective on his Life and Work*, he left behind football so entirely that, if the World Cup happened to come on, he wouldn't even know who was playing.

What had originally attracted Mahfouz to the sport was not simply the beauty of the game—although there must have been that—but how it stood as a contest between nations. As a boy, he was taken to a match between the Egyptian and English teams, and the Egyptians won. "Until then," he says, "I had thought the English were invincible, even in sports."

In her short essay on why football is like writing (and why writing is like football), Lebanese author Maya al-Hajj echoes these sentiments, writing that football "restores the voices of countries that have been silenced by the great empires. Football shuffles the cards that have been arranged by the major powers, allowing those on the margins to experience a happiness that has otherwise been lost in this harsh, hectic world."

Yet football is not always meritocratic. It has also been a plaything in the hands of autocrats and kings, as Yassin Adnan writes in "Matters of National Football." After the 1984 popular uprising in Morocco, in which Marrakeshi students were a leading force, the city's football club suddenly found itself being granted penalties left and right, until the team became the league champion, "with some honors that were deserved, and some that were achieved by other means."

Mina Ibrahim explores other ways in which government, military, and corporate forces have changed the game. In his essay "An Archive for Egyptian Football," Ibrahim writes about how much Egypt's neighborhood teams have been pushed aside to make way for corporate teams, such as teams for a petroleum company (Enppi), a bank (al-Bank al-Ahly), and a ceramics company (Ceramica Cleopatra). The football he knew as a boy is rapidly disappearing, and Ibrahim calls for a national archive project to preserve the knowledge and insights of fans. Ibrahim also writes movingly about those who died in stadium massacres in 2012 and 2015, and how he wrote, in his diary, that he would never to go to a game alone again: "I should be accompanied by a friend or a relative, so if I die, I could find someone next to me."

Mahfouz was not the only writer who might have risen to football greatness. Syrian author Lukman Derky also played the sport. Here, in four texts translated by Daniel Behar, Derky explores the sport with a satiric edge. In "Knocking on Blue Freedom's Door," he recounts a match that his neighborhood team played against the team at the Aleppo Central Prison. Other contributors also write about football with a dark humor. The anonymous "Iraqi Shalash" sardonically narrates his neighbor's gun-happy attitude toward football fandom, while Saudi author Hatem Alzahrani's poem "Fort-Da," translated by Moneera Al-Ghader, addresses the litterati who over-intellectualize the game, the one who "adjusts his glasses, gargles with elegant words, / then addresses the masses" about the sport.

Leonie Rau has brought together a section of football chants from five countries, with chants that are taunting, uplifting, and sharply critical of local governments. This section brings a range of songs, from a 2019 Algerian chant that became an anthem of the protest movement that ended the presidency of Abdelaziz Bouteflika, to a chant from the Hilal al-Quds club in East Jerusalem, which declares, "Olé, olé, olé, olé / Freedom, and Jerusalem will stay Arab."

Although as Naguib Mahfouz and Mina Ibrahim both observed, football has become big business, the short fiction for this issue, interestingly, leans toward a focus on childhood. Short stories by Adania Shibli, Yasmeen Hanoosh, and Ameer Hamad all foregrounding the dreams and disappointments of young players. Indeed, there is something eternally nascent about a passion for football, always coming into being, with the wide possibilities of youth.

Lastly, some may wonder why we refer to the great game as "football" when spellings in this magazine are otherwise US American. We jointly decided that the word football is not only the better echo of كرة القدم, but that the word also has deeper linguistic roots and greater breadth of use, moving more effortlessly between countries, slipping past defenders and, like an "Aquila" shot in Ameer Hamad's "Captain Rabeh," soars like an Arab eagle into the sky, before it descends to tear into the net.

Photo: Elba Mountain, Egypt ©WikiCommons

Previous spread:
Somalia
Above: Dubai, UAE
Left: Fayoum, Egypt
© Rawpixel, Unsplash,
WikiCommons

Left: Somalia
©*Rawpixel*
Below: Tunisia
© *Unsplash, Tine Boujemil*

Left: Jordan,
© Yazan Obeidat, Unsplash
Right: Egypt
©WikiCommons

Left: Turkey
©Unsplash
Above: Somalia,
© Rawpixel
Next spread: Egypt
©WikiCommons

۱۸
18

Excerpt

Knocking on Freedom's Door

Four Football Pieces | By **Luqman Derky**

Translated by Daniel Behar

A Note from the Translator

Luqman Derky (1966-) is a Kurdish-Syrian poet, actor, dissident blogger and cultural organizer from the town of Darbasiya on the Turkish-Syrian border. He now lives in France. In the context of a football issue, the autobiographical story behind this poem is worth recounting, as told on Derky's personal blog*. It reveals that Derky is not only a poet and actor but also a gifted amateur futbulji who, under slightly different circumstances, could well have started a professional career.

Derky used to play in neighborhood leagues and was frequently found running on the pitch at Aleppo College. One day, a friend came there to rush him over to the city stadium. Without his knowledge, Derky had been entered into the roster of the Hurriyya U-20 professional football club. He was numbered among the starting eleven for their crucial match against Ittihad. Derky describes

Derky's personal blog

walking into the locker room as if stepping into the Holy of Holies. He looks wide-eyed at the uniforms and the gorgeous green football socks to which the poem refers. He is handed—God Almighty!—a pair of authentic Adidas cleats. A teen footballer from Aleppo's poor neighborhoods could only fantasize of real cleats! Playing on asphalt, the kids would wear shoes mockingly called *adidas abu riha*: a cheap knock-off which, as its moniker suggests, was primarily efficient in absorbing foot odors.

Derky recounts the indelible shock of stepping onto a real football pitch with 40,000 spectators watching. Because of the intense rivalry among Aleppo football clubs, there were actually 40,000 people (30,000 Ittihad fans and 10,000 Hurriyya) in attendance for an under-twenty derby. Derky remembers the terror and awe of hearing the chorus of thirty thousand shouting in unison: "*ukhtek ala ummek, Hurriyya!*" (Hurriyya, your sister fucks your mom!). He played formidably as a center-back sweeper and helped the team keep a clean sheet to gain a 1-0 triumph. He also brought a poetic sensibility to bear on his defensive role by assuming its archaically romantic title: *libero*, from the Italian "free." The *libero* is the spare defender who may either form the last line of defense or advance to thicken the midfield.

Among the forty thousand fans, there was one very distinguished guest: Coach Ibrahimov, head coach of the Syrian U-20 national team. The coach was so impressed with Derky that he summoned him to the national squad that made the group round of the 1989 FIFA U-20 World Cup held in Saudi Arabia. Syria played in the group assigned to the stadium in Dammam. Two losses against the Soviet Union and Colombia prevented the team from advancing to the next stage. But they gave a strong display in a remarkable 3-1 victory against Costa Rica, which was enough to make them a media sensation back home. Derky vividly recalls the lavish praise and luxuries showered on them as an astonishing anomaly in a country used to all manner of tight-fisted austerity. Upon return, they were received by a high-ranking Baath official. Derky noticed the coach pointing him out to this official. He was frightened that he was about to be punished for underperforming. But the official approached smilingly, patted Derky on the back, and congratulated him: "*bravo alek*, you lifted your country's pride." Derky laughed to himself secretly: "If only he knew who I really am…"

Adel Qafu, head coach of our amateur team, informed us that we were heading to Aleppo Central Prison in Muslimiyya to face the prison's team. We all cheered together for this precious, rare encounter. Our goalkeeper, Abdu Qafu, told us about the strong friendships he maintained with some of the experienced criminals there and how he planned to make them gather crowds to root for us against our opponent. But how?

Knocking on Blue Freedom's Door

"Do the players belong to the police force or the thieves?" one of our failed players asked. "The thieves, you moron," our always-angry coach said. Our bus was setting out. Half of the players on the bus belonged to the Qafu clan, while the other half came from our neighborhood, Salah al-Din.

My friend Abdu Qafu was the team's joker. Usually, he played goalkeeper; under pressure, he stood as a formidable center-back; in moments of desperation for a goal, he would come forward to attack, and when chaos reigned, you would find him in midfield. He had played for professional clubs—al-Hurriyya, al-Jalaa, al-'Ummal [1]—but the neighborhood amateur teams always appealed to him more.

[1] All three are Aleppo-based football clubs.

Our team's name was al-Shahbaa [2] and we were ranked in the second division of the amateur league. Nothing out of the ordinary here. The league of non-professional neighborhood teams is an organized affair formed in two divisions, with the possibility of relegation and qualification for the upper division. We were engaged in a qualification battle for the upper division. It was our natural place, which we had lost two years back. Our pre-season preparations thus necessitated a number of friendly matches. The match in Neirab Camp ended in a scuffle in which all the tough guys on our team took part. I was later accused of cowardice because I tried to break up the fight.

[2] "The Grey One", a common epithet for the city of Aleppo.

When playing on neighborhood teams, you had to acquire karate skills first, football skills second. Instead of carrying red and yellow cards, the refs carry pocket-knives for protection. A referee in these matches will have a fifty-percent chance of getting beaten up by either the players or the spectators. No wonder the crowds show up; more often than not, it's to watch the fights rather than the football match.

The historical record of the Aleppo College football field shows that Kambris, a famous referee, never left a match he officiated without causing a ruckus. Naturally, he suffered his share of scratches, bruises, and wounds but he never once declined an offer to officiate matches, even as far as Kafr Hamra or al-Safira. Officiating ran in Kambris's blood, and it was in his nature to make bad calls that incited not only controversies but brawls. There is no room for debating an unpalatable decision in amateur league matches. The cost of a penalty call will be a grinding skirmish that, with any luck, will last only fifteen minutes until cool-headed members of the coaching staff and audience prevail in coming between the brawlers. But if the fight lasts longer than fifteen minutes, forget about it: you can kiss the match goodbye and stand by as the crowds rush into a free-for-all battleground.

Anyhow, to be brief, after giving our IDs to the guards, we entered the prison for the friendly match against the prisoners' team. We were welcomed by the prison warden, members of the team and their coach, a prison officer. As matter of course, the warden gave us a lecture, calmly at first, about the importance of sports. He cited the words of the eternal leader Hafez al-Assad— "It is my belief that sports equals life"—and stirred himself up, using threats and warnings for those who were tempted to deviate from the leader's text. When he spoke, I saw myself for a moment as a prisoner, and I was scared of being thrown in jail if we committed some error. But the whistle blew, and the match began.

The pitch was shitty asphalt. It was surrounded on all sides by the prisoners who were slamming us with foul language of the kind construction workers aim at young women. I got a fair share of their mouthfuls. They would call me Hajj Laklak and point to my slender calves that resembled stork legs.

I was positioned as a right-winger and contended with the left-back Rahmu, who graciously introduced himself as serving a life sentence for premeditated homicide, so I better beware of playing tricks on him. My friend Zakkur, who played center forward, was destined to come up against their center-back Shamandi who, by his own account, faced charges of child rape. It was a friendly match of pure terror. I managed to slip in between defenders and face off with a goalkeeper whose face was covered in slashes both horizontal and vertical. As soon as I shot the ball into the net and scored our first goal, the prisoners' head coach, a police officer, ran down to the pitch with the coaching crew, slapped the goalkeeper's face, and ordered him to be substituted.

As the new keeper walked into the court, the substituted keeper walked out, probably heading to solitary confinement with curses and dreams of revenge: "I will show you, Hajj Laklak." The strikers of the prisoners' team then scored four straight goals into the back of Abdu's net, all illegal. We did not dare protest. The child rapist center-back was groping Zakkur for no apparent reason. We stepped off the pitch defeated, and on the way out, shook hands with our opponents in a fine display of sportsmanship.

Despite the illegality of the four goals, we did not complain to the referee. We drank tea with the prison warden, then took a tour of the wards. In the prison library, I noticed there were three copies of Bertolt Brecht's play *The Days of the Commune*. Why shouldn't I steal one? No harm to the prisoners… I grabbed one and placed it, with true sportsmanship, in the bag with my team uniform. Before we left, a policeman stamped the back of our hands with the prison's blue seal to authorize our exit from the premises. We raised our hands to the guard's door to show our blue seals, took our leave and uttered a sigh of relief. As I left, I chanted to myself a variation on the verse by Ahmad Shawqi: "Blue freedom has a door open / to every stamped hand that comes knocking." **3**

Originally published in *Raseef 22*, June 30, 2017.

---

3 *The original beit by Egyptian neo-classical poet Ahmad Shawqi runs as follows: "And red freedom has a door open / to every stained hand that comes knocking." The line was recited in Cairo as part of a qasida composed in response to the French 1925 bombing of Damascus and intended to confer heroic value on the lives of the Syrian fallen.*

Syrians on the Pitch

4 *Nihad Qal'i played opposite Duraid Lahham's in several movies and TV shows. His character, the mild, slightly gullible Husni al-Barozan often fell prey to the tricks of Ghawwar, the role for which Lahham was made famous.*

In the mid-1980s of the previous century, we would go to the Aleppo university campus and play football on a small dirt pitch the size of five-against-five with a goalie. We would go there as a team to meet other teams representing the various districts of Syria or, to be precise, the resident students on university campuses in other districts.

In addition to Syrian teams, there was also a team of Eritrean students who had a remarkable playing style of sharing the ball among themselves as opposed to us Syrians. We were like that gang from '*kull min ido ilo*' ('where the most violent one prevails'), the fictive neighborhood invented by comedian Nihad Qal'i (or Husni al-Barozan, the character he played). **4** Most times, we would leave the court with voices hoarse from shouting at whomever on our team was hogging the ball, imploring him to make a pass. Whereas the Eritreans would, by silent agreement, pass fluently from one player to another.

One time, as chance would have it, the Eritreans came with an extra player. Coincidentally, at the same time, our team was missing someone. We decided to let the Eritrean Anwar play with us rather than sit on the reserves bench. Anwar was very happy with our kind offer and started playing on our team. As usual, when the Eritreans held possession, they passed the ball around until one of us managed to intercept a pass and we began yelling in his direction: "pass, ya Abdu.. pass it forward.. see me on your left, Abdu," etc. But Abdu didn't listen. He rushed forward planlessly, advanced the ball and tricked his way past one player. We raised our voices higher: "give it up already! make a pass!" but in vain. Abdu would not heed anyone. He lost the ball, fell on the ground, pretended to be injured and got up as if nothing happened.

Once again, the Eritreans were practicing their regular ball movement. This time, Mahmud managed to snatch the ball from the legs of our Eritrean brothers. He held onto it hard, my friends, so we began to scream: "pass the ball, Mahmud.. pass it forward." But Mahmud didn't listen either. It is here that Anwar, the Eritrean who played for us, learned that there was no other way but screaming. So, he began to scream. "Make a pass, brother Mahmud.. pass the ball, mate!" But our pal Mahmud was a very obstinate ball-hog and the ball was with him now. He got past one player, weaseled past another and then, alas, the Eritrean team took the ball away. Now our fellow Eritreans had the ball. Their passing dynamo was working non-stop, tic-tac-toe, until we were slapped with a goal that, as they say, put us in the orphanage.

We resumed the game from centerfield, friends, and Abu Ahmad got hold of the ball. In a 'kill or be killed' mode, he ran it forward. He wanted to score no matter what. Anwar haphazardly joined the attack on the right, but Abu Ahmad continued solo. Anwar shouted at him: "pass the ball, mate, make a pass.. Abu Ahmad!" But our pal Abu Ahmad wanted to score alone. To pass up the ball, to open up the game—that was unthinkable! His kick went well wide of the net. Too bad! Here Anwar rose up in protest: "you people… why don't you share the ball with me? Is this about skin color?" I approached him and said: "why do you think you're so special, my dear Anwar? Are you accusing us of racism?!!" "Yes, I am," said Anwar, "Why else would you not pass me the ball?" I stared at him fiercely and said: "Can you name one time when one Syrian player on this team passed the ball to another Syrian?" Anwar took a while to ruminate and replay the match in his head. He then said: "I apologize, friend. My judgment was hasty. You guys are not racist. But honestly, you are something much, much worse…"

From Derky's storytelling blog *Alf Sarda wa-Sarda*. Posted to his public Facebook page on June 20, 2021.

In a depressing restaurant
it's me and my friend, the melancholic poetician
I ask the waiter for a glass of water
he brings it over and says:
"this glass of water is for the sake of Hurriyya"
another one chimes in and says:
"for the precious eyes of Hurriyya, everything on the house"
another waitress, a wretched-looking old woman, tells me:
"everyone here is a big fan of Hurriyya."
We take off, myself and my poeticizing, befuddled friend
who is now loaded with hopes and romantic dreams
we take off while I keep thinking
that all the employees in this restaurant, by odd coincidence,
root for Huriyya football club. [5]

"Laterna," Damascus, 21/10/1998

[5] *The twist ending reveals the pun that runs through the poem: al-Hurriyya is both "liberty, freedom" and the name of an Aleppo football club. The club is primarily associated with Hayy al-Siryan, the Syriac neighborhood, and its mix of ethnic minorities: Assyrian Christians, Armenians, Kurds, Greeks and Circassians.*

Forty Thousand Spectators

Forty thousand spectators are rooting for the red team
And I alone am rooting for the green team
Forty thousand
Gasping, screaming, roaring
Every time a ball strikes my team's goalpost
Or the keeper collects the ball
Every time there is a scoring chance or a counterattack.
I alone cannot jump up
Every time we have a dangerous freekick
I cannot applaud
For an elegant attack performed by my team.
Then my team scores a goal
I neither jump up nor scream out of fear of them
And my team scores again
I show no excitement
Because they are forty thousand
and can crush me in a flash of anger.
The game ends
The forty thousand leave the stadium in a ruckus
Swearing at everything
Kicking stones on the way back
And I cry
They pat my shoulder
Thinking that I
Am more loyal than they are to their losing team.

Poetry

Fort-Da

By Hatem Alzahrani

Translated by
Moneera Al-Ghadeer

كُرة ... قَدم

Originally published in
Celebrating the Dual at Yale.
Dar Tashkeel, 2019

A Note from the Translator

While the poem is richly replete with theoretical insinuations, it inadvertently rolls into a metapsychological realm by evoking "Freudian temptation" as it stages the intellectual's compulsive play and illusion of a "sense of mastery" over his game. This indicates that translation is a theoretical reading of the specters that haunt the text and calls for a retranslation of other poetic and metaphorical registers centered on this haunting. The poem complicates the reading of the transitional object in question—football in poetry—as the intellectual slides into the scene of the "fort-da" game discussed by Freud in *Beyond the Pleasure Principle*. Simply put, Freud's one-and-a-half-year-old grandson Ernst has a wooden reel which he throws away, saying "o-o-o," before pulling on the string and murmuring "da" as a way to compensate for his mother's absence. Freud and the boy's mother, Sophie, interpret the first sound as indicating the German "fort," meaning "gone away," and the second sound, "da," as indicating "there" or "there it is."

For Freud, the child's play is an attempt to maintain mastery over a traumatic event of separation and loss. Such play prepares us for the losses that will mark our lives and is interestingly generated in the margins of the intellectual's dilemma with speech and silence as well as in his ambivalent relationship with the masses. Similarly, the poem illustrates the poet's limitation in the scene of writing that is already marked by language's infinite movement between here and there, presence and absence. It is here where the poem stages its playful trope that matches the repetition of "football," "ball," "players," and "play," amusingly suggesting that "fort-da" is the first psychoanalytic scene of "football."

I love the intellectual
as he rationalizes his Freudian temptation
with old players:

he adjusts his glasses, gargles with elegant words,
then addresses the masses

(who labor more than he does
and are free of groundless concepts):

"There is a strong Marxist conflict
in which immigrants
rise from the margins of the text; appear as
a battle waged by wealthy real estate agents
against the traditional power center
in the capital."

Dear eloquent one,
you have the right to enjoy the appeal behind the bookshelves,
and time has a space for bleak visions

I fear, for you, the fear of your own desires.
Don't be concerned with interpretation,
practice your human simplicity,
and let the soccer balls roll on the lawn
(words won't play while they are together)
then sing
or be quiet for a while

and if you won't, then speak,
speak so we cannot see you,
for you are filled by others,
and your name is at the end of the list!

احب المثقف
وهو يبرر فتنته الفرويدية
باللاعبين القدامى:

يعدل نظارته
يغرغر بالكلمات الأنيقة
ثم يتقول لعامّته
(المنتحبين على الأرض أكثر منه
وبدون مفاهيم مقطوعة القدمين):

"هنالك صراعٌ قوي ماركسي
على الذو يبدي الطريق الهامشي
من هامش النص
معركة تشنُّها الربا العقار الثرية
على مركز السلطة التقليدية
في العاصمة."

عزيزي الأنيق:
لك الحق أن تتمتع بالجاذبية خلف الرفوف
وفي الوقت متسعٌ للرؤى القاتمة

أخاف عليك من الخوف من رغباتك
لا تنشغل بالتأويل
مارس بساطتك البشرية
اترك كرات العشب يلعبن
(لن تلعب الكلمات وهنّ مَعَا)
ثم غنّ
أو اصمت قليلاً

وإنْ لم تفعل فتكلم
تكلم بلا نراك
فأنتَ الممتلئ بالآخرين
واسمك في الآخر القائمة!

Essay

How Football Is Like Writing & Writing Is Like Football

Curated by **Huda al-Daghfaq**

Translated by Anam Zafar

Only the uninitiated forget the fun and focus on results

Wahid Al Tawila

Perhaps the common denominator between football and writing is that both are primarily looking to entertain. Of course, there are those who want results, too—they are the ones who created the idea of the fanatic, whether for a football team or a writer. This repulsive fanaticism has produced writers who win prizes even though most of their writing is devoid of any enjoyment. And just as there are idiotic referees, there are also idiotic critics. Sometimes, referees can incorrectly judge offenses that occur on the pitch, or even fail to see them at all. But that should not happen with a literary critic.

With a clever manager, even a football team with the most meticulous plan can still change that plan if the match's circumstances require it. The novelist has a plan, too, which could also change depending on how the novel plays out and what the character wants—never mind what the novelist wants. Similarly, in football, the manager isn't always in control. But this requires a striker of Romário's caliber, whose manager simply can't predict what he will do, even if his overactive imagination makes him think he can. As for defenders, most find their powers of imagination only in rare cases, no matter how skilled they are. Baresi was excellent but had no imagination. Even Beckenbauer had none. I hate all defenders, except in the rare cases of the Moroccan players Dolmy and El Biyaz.

Do you know the story of the Egyptian player Magdi Abdelghani, also known as Magdi Maqasheh? Nándor Hidegkuti was managing Al Ahly football club at the time. At the end of training, he would split the players into two teams—a red team and a white team—for a practice match. With no space left on the teams, the remaining players became substitutes, each assigned to somebody on the pitch. However,

ABDEL-GHANY

Maqasheh would not accept being consigned to the substitute bench. He would pace up and down, waiting for another player to get injured. Eventually, someone did pick up an injury, and he proceeded onto the pitch in their place. From that day on, he didn't leave the pitch, come hell or high water.
People like Maqasheh are the kind who write thirty novels: ready to do anything except show a hint of real creativity. Creativity requires imagination. The former Dutch player Van Basten, for example, is extremely creative, despite having only one novel to his name. We need novelists from the same mold as Cruyff, the Dutch football player, and Bettega, from Italy; both were talented, but didn't win any awards, so they were forgotten… They are the Sabri Moussa of football.

Football and writing also share the need for a plan and the distribution of roles. Contemporary novels, and contemporary football, have begun to use the same tactics: on the pitch, the defenders have started to attack; on the page, the secondary characters may be the ones to stay on your mind, with the main character retreating to make way for them. In football, you can't play without defenders; in a novel, this is possible: your game can consist solely of attacking. In football, you can't play without a goalkeeper; in a novel, you can, only to find that you have made yourself vulnerable to attacks from critics. In football, you can play like Italy: defending in the first rounds, then attacking once you reach the quarterfinals. In a novel, this technique is painful—even if it is a winner for Italy, a team that actually manages to defend creatively. In football, the crazed crowd will forget a terrible beginning so long as their team wins in the end. In a novel, your crowd won't wait for you and they won't forgive you—even if they did forgive Faulkner. The one thing that might bring them comfort is if you win a prize, even an inferior prize, which is the worst thing that could happen. That is because the fanatics and the uninitiated forget the fun and remember only the results.

Finally, both football and writing take pleasure in calculated attacks. Defending and attacking at the right times ensures a plan isn't exposed too early. Some novels focus on zone defense, and then attack at the end. In this case, the defense needs to be enjoyable, so the reader doesn't run away, and the spectator doesn't die of boredom. Counterattacks require two clever characters who can score the goal before resubmitting to the rules.

Maqasheh scoring from point against Netherlands, 1990
© YouTube

Continued on page 36

Some offsides go unaccounted

Raouf Musad

In football stands around the world, thousands of people of all nationalities gather with their drums and their flags, roaring in approval—or disapproval—at a player's attitude or a referee's whistle, while millions of others crowd around their television sets to watch the same matches, hoping for one team to outperform the other. Around the globe, millions follow this festive ritual that has its own rules, priests, and temples. If any person stood in the middle of any square in any city of the world to sing the praises of Mohamed Salah or Cristiano Ronaldo, everyone within earshot would join in. But if they did the same with Naguib Mahfouz, only certain groups of people would respond.

That is the big difference between football players and writers; even if a writer wins the most prestigious international prizes, most of the world still won't know their name. This wouldn't happen with a football player.

On the football pitch, there are rules, whereas writing has none. For example, while it's nigh on impossible to agree whether one writer really has gone offside to steal another's ideas, a football player must steal the ball to shoot it into the opponent's net. And while football players must cooperate and interact in a way that forms a cohesive team, writers cannot do this. Each writer works on their own, with their own writing style. The set rules of football cannot be violated, but writers might create new literary rules through their work, which other writers and critics can draw from. In other words, writers can put the cart before the horse, and have no obligation to step in the same river twice.

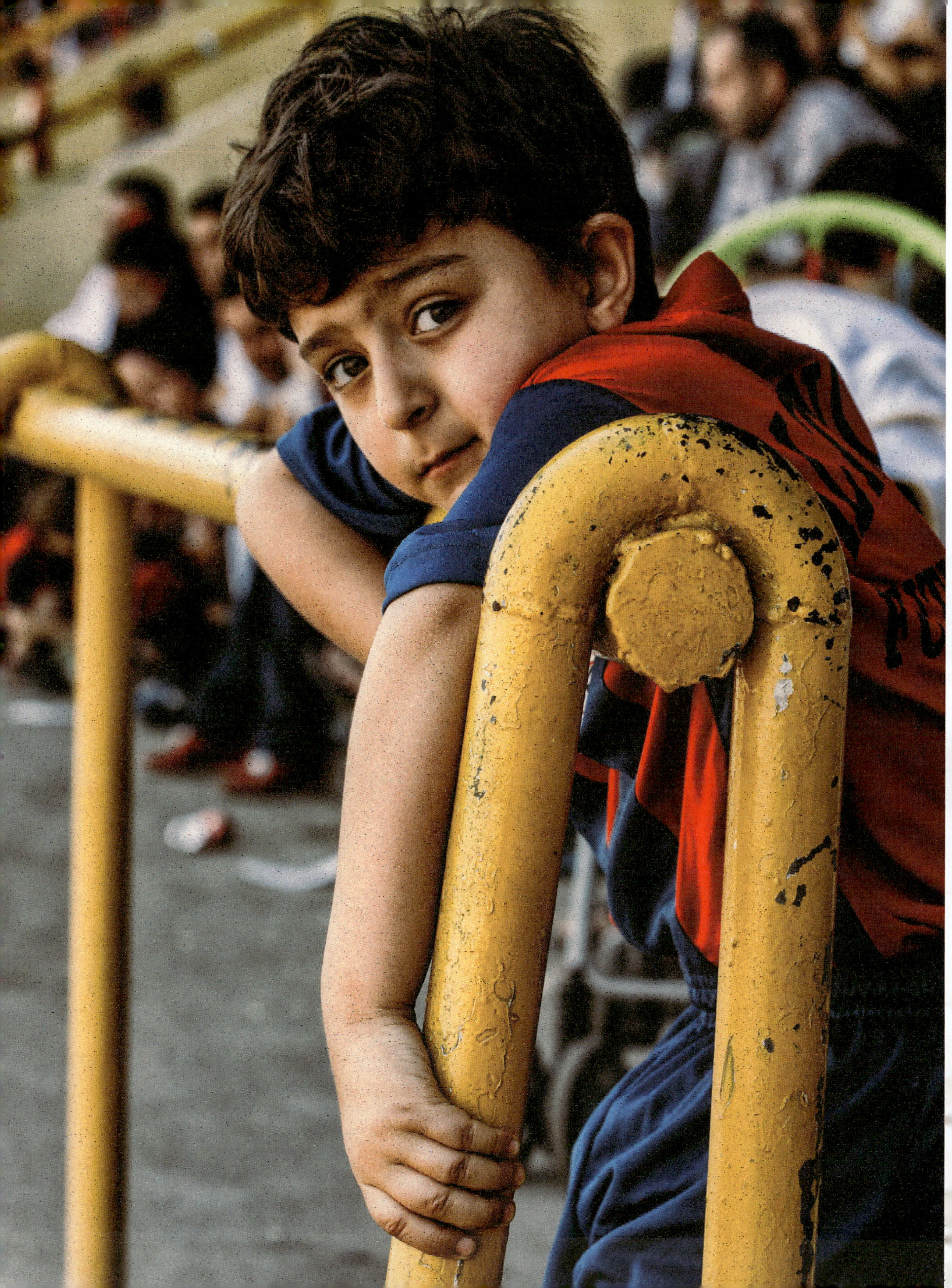

Darwish wrote about Maradona

Maya al-Hajj

I really find it strange, the way Arab literary figures look down on topics such as sport, folklore, and fashion with an air of unjustified superiority. As the French writer Stendhal says in his definition of the novel, the core purpose of literature is to reflect our lives back to us, as if the writer is carrying a mirror with them along the way. Writing novels has become limited to fixed topics such as love, homeland, and identity, while other—supposedly inferior—topics have disappeared. But some writers, whether novelists, poets, or thinkers, broke these senseless literary principles in order to broach issues considered to be on the creative margins.

For example, Edward Said wrote an article about the Egyptian belly dancer and actor Tahiya Carioca, in which he argued that belly dancing remained a prisoner of the male gaze. Elsewhere, following Argentina's win in the 1986 World Cup, Mahmoud Darwish wrote a poem about Diego Maradona in which he asked: "Why is football not a topic of art and literature?" It wasn't a strange question, since Darwish had lived in Europe and observed how the continent—from regular citizens to literary figures and politicians—had an avid interest in the sport. Even the greatest thinkers mentioned football in their books and articles, including Albert Camus, who described the haters of the sport as "stupid." In the past few years, I have read some new literary works which take football as their main subject. These include Ahmad Mohsin's *Sani' al-Al'aab* and Shukri Mabkhout's *Baghanda*. Personally, I have always been very fond of the sport. It is a game that conquers people's thoughts and emotions, placing them under great pressure and leading to either overwhelming happiness or grievous disappointment at the end of the match. I used to love how the star players of a match could completely transform our spirits, even if we were watching from another continent. It is no secret that, in my teenage years, I preferred football players to film and music stars, with a particular admiration for David Beckham, Luís Figo, Raúl González, Trézéguet, and Cannavaro.

There is a collective magic that this sport casts over the world. It creates stars out of poor boys and restores the voices of countries that have been silenced by the great empires. Football shuffles the cards that have been arranged by the major powers, allowing those on the margins to experience a happiness that has otherwise been lost in this harsh, hectic world. Yes, it's just a game, but it is also a representation of life. From the outside, you see a pitch, players, and referees. But in reality, many others are involved behind the scenes, from world leaders and politicians to mobsters and wealthy elites. Still, at the end of the day, all we really care about is that fleeting joy offered to us by heroes from around the world, all running behind a single ball.

First published in Alfaisal magazine in May 2018.

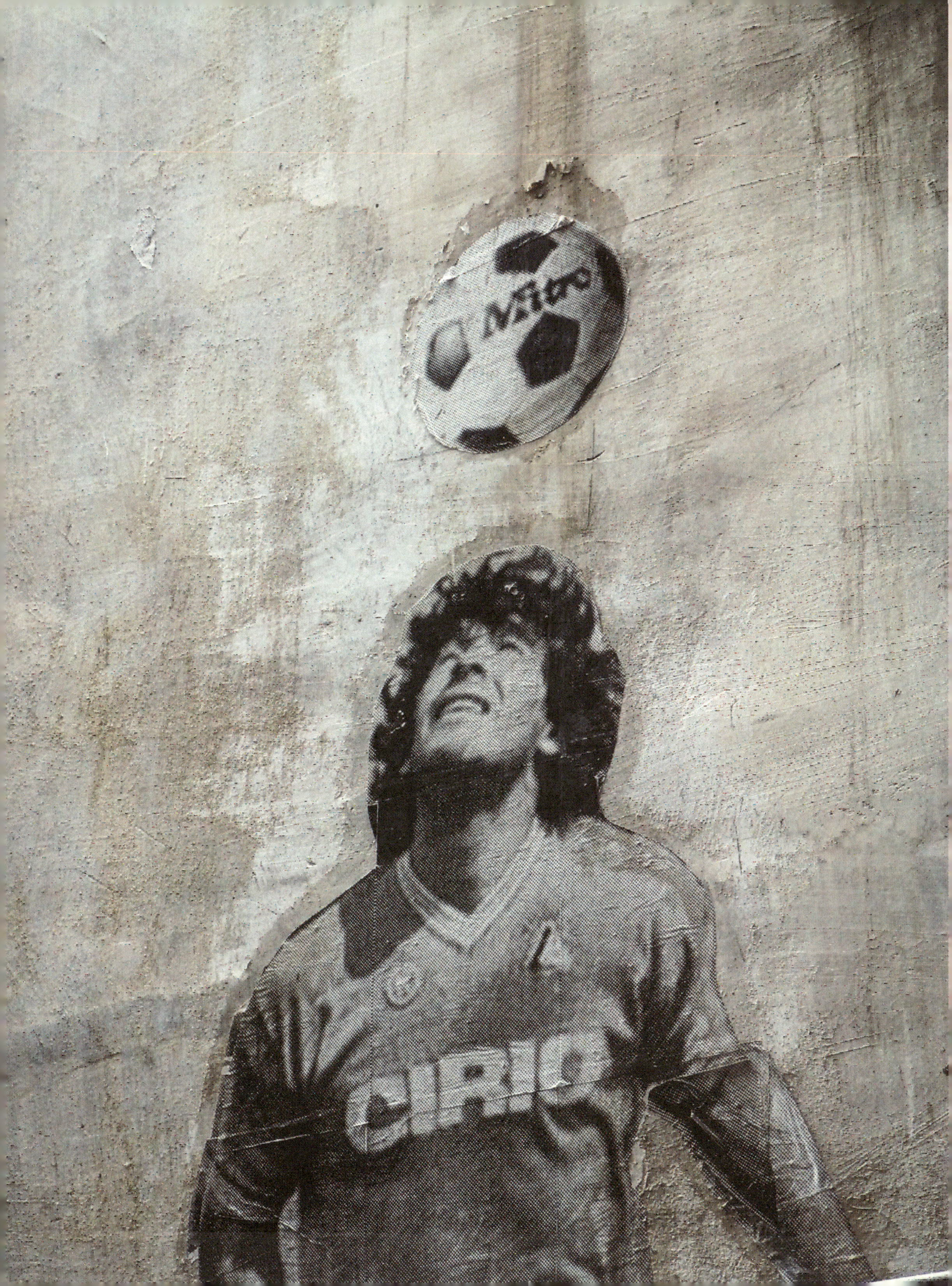
Mitre
CIRIO

Poetry

With a Hoarse Voice

Football Chants from Five Countries

The old adage that football is "just a game" has never been true for its fans, and the saying falls particularly flat in recent years, when football fans have taken an enormous role in political, societal, and humanitarian causes. As Ronnie Close describes in his book *Cairo's Ultras*, "chants and songs heighten the atmosphere to create formidable soundscapes and explosive visual forces, fused into communal ecstatic experiences with Sufi traces that have surpassed the standard for sporting competitions."

Here, we have collected football chants from five Maghrebi and Mashreqi countries, from Morocco to Bahrain, expressing love, frustration, protest, and anger, combining the emotional forces of music and football.

Edited by **Leonie Rau**

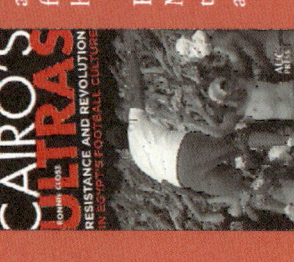

ALGERIA

Ouled El Bahdja – La Casa d'El Mouradia

This football song, composed by the USMA fan collective Ouled El Bahdja, became an anthem of the 2019 protest movement that ended the presidency of Abdelaziz Bouteflika in Algeria. El Mouradia is the presidential residence; the title alludes to the Spanish crime drama La Casa␣de␣Papel (Money Heist).

Selected & translated by Lameen Souag

Hours to dawn and I still haven't slept,
I'm taking drugs, but only bit by bit;
Who's the cause, who should I blame?
We're fed up with this life.

In the first term, we'd say it's fine;
They tricked us with the decade [of civil war].
In the second, the story became clear—
La Casa d'El Mouradia.
In the third, the country got thin
thanks to private interests.
In the fourth, the doll [of a president] died
And the situation continued.

Hours to dawn and I still haven't slept,
I'm taking drugs, but only bit by bit;
Who's the cause, who should I blame?
We're fed up with this life.

The fifth term is following on,
It's been set up between them;
The past is archived,
The voice of freedom.
Our stand is for private talk,
They know him when he vomits;
A school where you need a CV,
An anti-illiteracy office.

Hours to dawn and I still haven't slept,
I'm taking drugs, but only bit by bit;
Who's the cause, who should I blame?
We're fed up with this life.

ساعات الفجر وما جاني نوم
راني نكونسومي غير بشوية
شكون السبة وشكون نلوم
ملينا العيشة هادي

فالأول نڨولو تڨولو جازت-حشاوهونا بالعشرية
La Casa Del Mouradia فالثانية الحكاية باتت شفاية
فالثالثة البلاد شيانت بالمصالح الشخصية
فالرابعة البوبية ماتت و مازالت القضية

ساعات الفجر وما جاني نوم
راني نكونسومي غير بشوية
شكون السبة وشكون نلوم
ملينا العيشة هادي

و الخامسة راي تسوڨي بيناتهم منية
و الباسي راو أرشيفي لا فوا تاع الحرية
فيراجنا العهدة برشي سخي بدو محو الڨبية
مدرسة و لازم سيفي و الخاسمة راي تسوڨي بيناتهم منية

ساعات الفجر وما جاني نوم
راني نكونسومي غير بشوية
شكون السبة وشكون نلوم
ملينا العيشة هادي

© Pexels

ALGERIA

Ouled El Bahdja – Babour ElLouh

The word *hogra* is part of the daily vocabulary of Algerians, expressing the bitterness of enduring a regime that oppresses and suppresses its people. Young Algerians have found clever ways of self-expression that transcend censorship. Through football chants, their collective echoing pains and frustrations have reached Algerians beyond the pitch. Ouled El Bahdja is a collective of USMA football fans that has embodied that resistance through self-expression since the 1990s. This chant reflects the intersections of football, politics, socioeconomics, migration, and the feelings of *hogra*. For those who want to escape the ills of the homeland, the wooden boat is often a symbol of their freedom.

Selected & translated by
Khadidja Bouchellia

I cannot bear this suffering
Time is fleeting
Whatever I do turns sour
though my intentions are good
this life is at an impasse

I say 'that's it'
But I make the same mistake over and over
Overthinking
has its hold on me
I say 'that's it'
But I make the same mistake over and over

Let me leave my heart is broken
Let me leave in the wooden boat
Let me leave my heart is broken
Let me leave in the wooden boat

Things are getting worse there's no solution
Distance is a must, and I must follow
I cannot come back, and you know why
You (Algeria) became a home for foreigners

مراني ش قادر نحمل هاذ لعذاب
الزمان راهو يطول علينا
ي ندير ها تمكسي
Pourtant نخدام صواب
هاذ ني ش ة العيش ة Impasse

ون قول خلاص
والغلطة نعاود ندير ها
fois 1000
هو ساي ي دار علينا
تعمار الراس
ون قول خلاص
والغلطة نعاود ندير ها
fois 1000

هو ساي ي دار علينا
تعمار الراس
خلين ي نروح قلب ي محروق
خلين ي نروح فبابور اللوح
خلين ي نروح قلب ي محروق
خلين ي نروح فبابور اللوح

لمكاين ة تكبر ماتقدياش حساب
لفراق نحتم زاد داق
مانقدرش نولي ، باك تعرف لجواب
مع ام خرجت ي عالبراني

| Studio | Live |

A mixing of genders
They wanted it this way
Build prisons
Women work while young men sleep
A mixing of genders
They wanted it this way
Build prisons
And women work while young men sleep

Let me leave my heart is broken
Let me leave in the wooden boat
Let me leave my heart is broken
Let me leave in the wooden boat

I am thinking hard
I am thinking of a good solution
To live at peace with myself
I have tirelessly tried
But only found failure
Awake an hour and oppressed a year

Those who escaped and made it
Their lives are long, and their path is written
Among honorable people
Very few are still holding on
Those who escaped and made it
Their lives long and their path written
Among honorable people
Very few are still holding on

Let me leave my heart is broken
Let me leave in the wooden boat
Let me leave my heart is broken
Let me leave in the wooden boat

تخلطوا اجناس
راي باينة هوما هكذا
ابني لحباس
هرا نخدم والشيبة راقدة
تخلطوا اجناس
راي باينة هوما هكذا
ابني لحباس
هرا نخدم والشيبة راقدة

خليني نروح قلبي مجروح
خليني نروح فباور اللوح
خليني نروح قلبي مجروح
خليني نروح فباور اللوح

نسبق في رايي
نخمم في حل شباب
بيني وبين روحي نعيش مهني
وشحال نحبا نسيي
l'échec غير شباب
ساعة صاحي وڤي عام مذني

لي سلك وحجاز
اعمار طويلة وطريقة كاتبة
والناس العزاز
حاجة قليلة لي مازالت شادة
لي سلك وحجاز
اعمار طويلة وطريقة كاتبة
والناس العزاز
حاجة قليلة لي مازالت شادة

خليني نروح قلبي مجروح
خليني نروح فباور اللوح
خليني نروح قلبي مجروح
خليني نروح فباور اللوح

USMA
OULED EL BAHDJA

Football theme

Maritime theme

The leader:
Why are you pissed off?
Why are you pissed off?
Who told you?
Who told you?
(The other team) has torn its clothes.

The audience:
Why aren't you speaking with me?
Why aren't you speaking with me?
To play around him?
To play around him?
(The other team) has torn its clothes.

مايحاچيني
مايحاچيني
ليش زعلان
ليش زعلان
من قايل لك
من قايل لك
تلعب عوده
تلعب عوده
(اسم الفريق) شقق ثيابه
(اسم الفريق) شقق ثيابه

BAHRAIN

Supporting Muharraq

The football chants of the Muharraq team are inspired by the seafaring songs recited during the days of pearl-diving. These songs are called *Nahma*, usually sung by pearl divers in the sea or during the rituals when the divers depart on long journeys. The chant begins with a *Nahma* song from Bahraini folklore. The first two lines are original, and they comprise prayers that support the Muharraq team. However, the second two lines provoke the other team: "I wished you farewell, the light of my eyes / Without you, my eyelids never covered my eyes. / You remained (the other team) a body without life, / Your mind escaped, and the body is lying down."

Selected & translated by
Hajar Mahfoodh

EGYPT

Ultras Ahlawy – Hekayetna

Selected by Mina Ibrahim & translated by Leonie Rau

Before we came, football was lies and deceit
It clouded minds and was a mask for the regime
They've tried to make it pretty, to keep it for the country:
And forgetting the stands filled with thousands
They would kill the idea, too,
Injustice is everywhere
I will never forget your past
You were a slave to the regime

When the revolution happened, we came out everywhere:
We came out for freedom and for the fall of those symbols of oppression
We won't shut up, we won't weaken, not as long as the regime exists:
The doggish police and oppression everywhere
They also kill the revolution
The word "free" drives them crazy
However much the jailor strikes out
Against my voice, he is a coward

We said it in the stands in front of millions:
Down with the regime that kills generations every day
They arranged a plot against us, the impossible:
They killed our dearest friends, they killed the dreams of many years

In Port Said, the victims saw betrayal before their deaths
They saw a regime that offered a choice between its reign and a country in chaos
The regime's idea was to one day rule alone
And for the revolutionaries to kneel to the military, as in the old days
Unleash more of your dogs
And chaos everywhere
I'll never give you my trust
And you'll never rule over me

In Port Said once the military opened the doors, the dogs
charged in, chaos spread, and they killed our dearest youth
Among them were engineers and workers and children
They died and their wish was for your rule to be cancelled
Oh Supreme Council, you bastards
For how much did you sell the martyrs' blood?
So you could protect the regime
That you, too, are part of

الكورة لما جينا كانت كذب و كانت خداع
كانت بغبية للعقول كانت قناع للبلاد
بيحاولوا يجملوها وتبقى لهم للبلاد:
وناسيين المدرج اللي مليئة ة بالآلاف
أقتل في الفكرة كمان
والظلم في كل مكان
عمري ما هنسالك زمان
كنت عبد للنظام

ولما الثورة قامت جينا في كل البلاد:
جينا على الحرية وسقوط رموز الفساد
موتنا على الحرية وسقوط رموز الفساد
مسكتناش ميدناش ما سا النظام موجود
داخلية الكلاب والظلم في كل مكان موجود
أقتل في الثورة كمان
كلمة حر تر بك جنان
مهما يريد يطش السجان
قدام صوتي بكون جبان

قولناها في المدرج قدام الملايين:
يسقط نظام بيقتل كل يوم في جيل وجيل
دبروا لنا الفؤامرة دبروا النا المستحيل:
قتلوا أغلى الصحاب قتلوا حلم السنين

في بورسعيد ضحايا شافوا الغدر قبل الممات
شافوا نظام خير ما بين حكمه والفوضى في البلاد
كان فاكر حكمه يوم هيحتاله في أعلى مكان
والشعب الثوري يركع للعسكر زي زمان
أطلق في كل مكان
والفوضى في كل مكان
عمري ما هديك الأمان
ولا تحكمنى يوم كمان

في بورسعيد العسكر فتحوا الباب
أطلقوا الكلاب فالعسكر فتحوا الباب
راحوا وكان مناهم يبرص حكمك لاغي في البلاد
منهم كان المهندس والعامل منهم ولاد
يا مجلس عسكر بكام
بعت دم شهيد بكام
علشان ما تحمي في النظام
اللي انت منه كمان

MOROCCO

RAJA Casablanca – F bladi delmouni
I Was Wronged in My Own Country

Selected & translated by Hicham Rafik

Oh oh oh oh
I was wronged in my own country
Oh oh oh oh
To whom shall I raise my grievance?
Oh oh oh oh
To the Lord Almighty
Oh oh oh oh
He, the only one who knows my sufferings

We live a miserable life in this country
We are seeking peace
Oh, our Lord, make us victorious
They killed us with drugs
And left us like orphans
We will seek revenge on Judgement Day
You wasted our youth's talents
And you destroyed them with drugs
As you always wanted it to be.
You sold our country's wealth
And gave it to foreigners
You repressed a whole generation

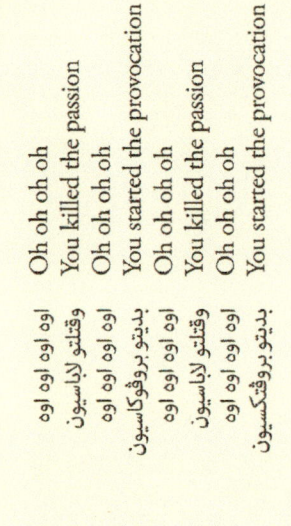

Oh oh oh oh
You killed the passion
Oh oh oh oh
You started the provocation
Oh oh oh oh
You killed the passion
Oh oh oh oh
You started the provocation

وه وه وه وه
فبلادي ظلموني
وه وه وه وه
لمن نشكي حالي
وه وه وه وه
الشكوى للرب العالي
وه وه وه وه
غير هو اللي داري

فهاد البلاد عايشين فقهامة طالبين السلامة
نصرنا يا مولانا
عرفو علينا حشيش كتامة خلاونا في اليتامى
كيف بغيتو تشوفوها
فلوس البلاد كع كليتوها للبراني عطيتوها
جيلنا سيون قهرتوها

وه وه وه وه
وقتلتو لباسيون
وه وه وه وه
بديتو بروفوكاسيون
وه وه وه وه
وقتلتو لباسيون
وه وه وه وه
بديتو بروفكسيون

No one feared what you invented,	زبرو خاف اللي اخترعتو وعلينا طبقتو
What you used on us	بيه بغيتو تحكمو
You just wanted to rule us	على فلذة حكمتو بالريكلو ومعى في تيفو
For a flare you sentenced us with Huis Clos, [1]	Les ultras t'arbo
You banned the Tifo [2]	بالشغب شحال تهمتو
You waged a war against the Ultras	نسيتو شحال صفقتو بشهور الحبس جازيتو
You accused us of inciting riots	رجاوي ضيعتو حياتو فخدمتو وقراتو
You forgot how much you applauded us	حيت ماقهمتو
Now you reward us with months in prison	la passion
You've ruined the Rajaouis' lives,	
Their jobs and their studies	
Because you didn't understand the meaning of passion	

Oh oh oh oh	اوا اوا اوا اوا
I'm sorry, my family	ديروا لقاصي
Oh oh oh oh	اوا اوا اوا اوا
The talk about me has become too much	علينا كثرو الهضاري
Oh oh oh oh	اوا اوا اوا اوا
It's getting on my nerves	الهضرة ق طلعات فراسي
Oh oh oh oh	اوا اوا اوا اوا
Just understand me already	وا غير فهموني

Every day the same speech	كل نهار نفس الهضرة
At home or in the streets:	فالدار ولا الزنقة وشنو عطاكم الخضرة
"What did Raja give to you?"	عمرك كلو ضاع عليها وشحال نفقتي عليها
"You lost your whole life for it."	يا حبابي غير فهموني ، علاش بغيتو تفرقوني
"So much money spent on it."	على الرجاء اللي نواسيني
"And never abandoned it."	هادي اخر كلمة عندي نكتبها من قلبي والدمعة ق عيني
My dear ones, just understand me	
Why do you want to separate me	
From Raja which consoles me?	
This is my final word	
Written from my heart	
With tears in my eyes	

Oh oh oh oh	اوا اوا اوا اوا
Repentance belongs to the Almighty	التوبة رب العالي
Oh oh oh oh	اوا اوا اوا اوا
Our Lord, accept our repentance	توب علينا يا ربي

1 French for behind closed doors, without an audience.

2 From the Italian, meaning the choreography often used by fans to support their team.

PALESTINE

Hapoel Umm al-Fahm FC – al-Hamra' Rayatna
Red Is Our Flag

Umm al-Fahm is a Palestinian city that was occupied in 1948. Thus, the residents of this city hold Israeli passports, and their team plays in the Israeli league. The city is like a Palestinian castle in Israel, against the Israeli policies and right-wing politics.

Selected & translated by Ameer Hamad

---

3 The second-highest football league in Israel.

4 Lajjun: A Palestinian village that was destroyed by Israel in 1948; an Israeli settlement was built in its place. Lajjun's people fled to Umm al-Fahm.

5 Meir Kahane and Baruch Marzel were two right-wing Israeli leaders.

6 The three Palestinian football trophies

Oh oh oh
Red is our flag
Oh oh oh
And victory is our goal

Since I was in elementary school
I've supported al-Fahmawiya
Wearing the team scarf and a Kufiyya

I come to you on Fridays
I pray for you
I sing for you

We are tired of the First Division 3
Our youth is wasted there
We'll qualify for Premier League!

No matter how long it takes us
We have raised the flag
The whole world is against us

Oh oh oh
Red is our flag
Oh oh oh
And victory is our goal

Fahmawy and your sons, oh Lajjun 4
Are worth the world to me
I will return to Lajjun no matter what

In the stands we raised our voices
We'll cheer until death
I'm Palestinian until death

In 1984
[Meir] Kahane and the right-wing
Went back disappointed

اوه اوه اوه
الحمر رايتنا
اوه اوه اوه
والنصر غايتنا

من وأنا بالابتدائية
شجعت الفحماوية
بالقحطة والكوفية

يوم الجمعة بأجيلك
بصلاش بدعيلك
وبغني بغنيلك

الدرجة الأول زهقناها
شبابنا ضيعناها
العليا راح نلاقها

لو مهما طالت علينا
الراية احنا علينا
كل العالم علينا

اوه اوه اوه
الحمر رايتنا
اوه اوه اوه
والنصر غايتنا

فحماوي وابنك يا اللجون
بتسوى عندي الكون
راجعلك شو ما يكون

بالمدرج علينا الصوت
بنشجع حتى الموت
فلسطيني للموت

سنة ال ٨٤
كهانا واليمين
رجعو خايبين

PALESTINE

Hilal Al-Quds Club – Hurriya
Freedom

Selected & translated by Ameer Hamad

مارزل أعاد وعد الكرّة
ما قدروها يفوتوا
أم الفحم يا حرّة

[Baruch] Marzel **5** tried again
They couldn't enter the city
Umm al-Fahm, the free one

اووه اووه
الحمر رايتنا
اووه اووه
والنصر غايتنا

Oh oh oh
Red is our flag
Oh oh oh
And victory is our goal

اولي اولي اولي اولي اولي
حريّة والقدس ح تفضل عربيّة

Olé, olé, olé, olé
Freedom, and Jerusalem will stay Arab

حريّة والأقصى والله في عينّي
حريّة الله هلال القدس عربيّة
اولي اولي اولي اولي اولي
حريّة إن شاء الله ح نوصل للقمّة
حريّة يلا يا هلال شدّ الهمّة
حريّة كل واحد فينا بسوى مئة

Freedom, al-Aqsa, by God, in my eyes
Freedom, God, Hilal, Jerusalem is Arab
Olé, olé, olé, olé
Freedom, inshallah we will reach the top
Freedom, yalla Hilal, be strong
Freedom, each of us has the strength of a hundred men

اولي اولي اولي اولي اولي
حريّة القدس والضفّة الغربيّة
حريّة هينا أخدنا الثلاثية **6**
فرحنا كل القدسيّة

Olé, olé, olé, olé
Freedom, Jerusalem, and the West Bank
Freedom, we won the treble **6**
We made all the Jerusalemites happy

اولي اولي اولي اولي اولي
حريّة بقلبي بروحي وبعيني
حريّة جيناكي بالهمّة القويّة
حريّة احنا الأسود الهلاليّة
اولي اولي اولي اولي اولي
اولي اولي اولي اولي اولي

Olé, olé, olé, olé
Freedom, I'll buy you with my spirit and my eyes
Freedom, we came to you with strong determination
Freedom, we are the Hilalian Lions
Olé, olé, olé, olé
Olé, olé, olé, olé

© Facebook

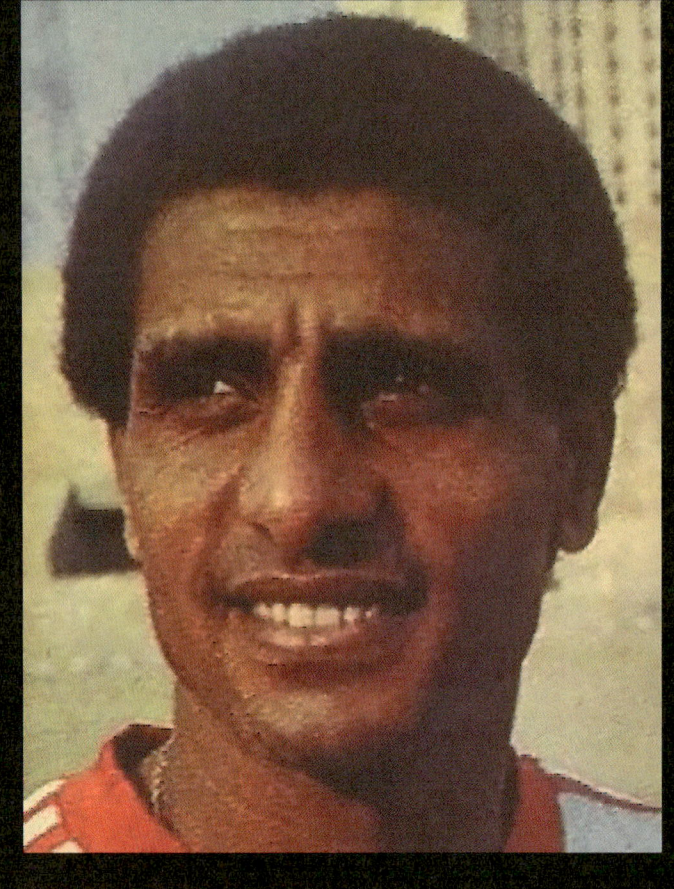

Farouk Gaafar as player for Zamalek SC and later as coach

The Archives

Farouk's Cosmos

An Almost Egyptian American Dream

By **Khaled Youssef**

Translated by
Becki Maddock

Hollis, Queens
© nooklyn.com

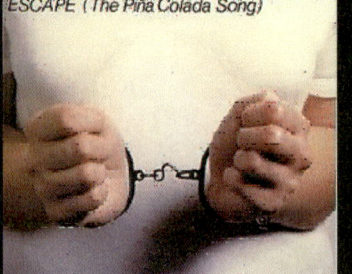

RUPERT HOLMES
ESCAPE (The Piña Colada Song)

```
I was tired of my lady
We'd been together too long
Like a worn out recording
Of a favorite song
...
```

For the first time it seemed pointless, and perhaps that was what made this the happiest moment of his time there, ever since his arrival more than three months before. His hair sprouted, unruly, from beneath the woolen sports cap. A pair of black gloves of the same brand showed signs of splitting, allowing his fingers to absorb the temperature, which was approaching two degrees below zero. He felt the frost through a hole in the gloves as he leaned gently on the metal wire fence, which separated his breath, disguised as white steam, and a deserted patch of land in the middle of the Hollis neighborhood in Queens. He has no idea that he's a few meters from the house of the teenage Darryl McDaniels, future member of the rap group Run-D.M.C. Farouk, who has just turned 28, senses the beginning of the end as the new decade dawns in Queens, missing even its ghosts, who have not yet returned from their New Year's parties and family gatherings. There are empty shops and a lone poster a couple of meters away from him for "Kramer vs. Kramer" (among all the posters that he came across, he notices this drama about a family conflict after the decision to separate). Even the ever-present open-air hot dog vendors on Jamaica Bay Boulevard have disappeared. Farouk, in contemporary parlance, is an illegal immigrant. He looks at the deserted patch of land, remembering details of yesterday's phone call home, including his deep sadness at learning details of his sister's worsening illness and feelings of extreme envy toward Hamama, who had scored two goals against Al Ittihad, the Alexandrian football team, two days ago in the Cairo stadium.

Run-DMC in a promotional shot. From left to right: Jason Mizell, Darryl McDaniels, and Joseph Simmons. WikiCommons

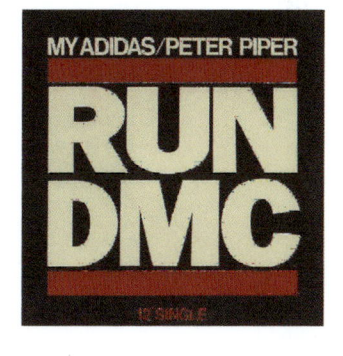

Fleeing the mistakes of his footballing era

Farouk was cocky, arrogant, egotistical, thin, weak-bodied, and materialistic. He wanted to leave behind his social class as soon as possible. He was popular, pretentious, talented, calm, troublesome; he shirked responsibility and was a malingerer in the closed circuits of the seventies. Music emanating from a single shop near the intersection with Myrtle Avenue broke into the monotony of the early morning hours. Robert Holmes' song "Escape," about a man who lives a monotonous married life responding to a message posted by one of the girls in the classified ads of a newspaper, addressed to any man who loves adventure, was calling him to immediate escape. Farouk did not know the details of the song, but one of his colleagues at Cosmos had given him a brief overview, which made him regret declaring his desire to know, just as it had upset him the previous September that Giorgio Moroder's song "Chase" from "Midnight Express" was blasting out in Rome airport, propagandizing him as an Egyptian as part of his plan to escape to America, leaving behind Zamalek and his colleagues in the Egyptian national team after participating in a training course for Mediterranean players in Split. His discomfort logically stemmed from a line in Holmes's song, that our life is "like a worn-out recording of a favorite song." Farouk knew only too well that he was not merely searching for adventure or a break from a monotonous life. He was fleeing from a feeling of constant judgment, from a situation in which he felt that judgment was reciprocal, and that escape was the just reward for a path that drank too much from the Egyptian moral dictionary without this translating into any real, material feelings of security. The suspension in April 1975 ignited those initial desires within Farouk: to enter the game with new rules, settling on a monthly contract of 150 pounds, and the

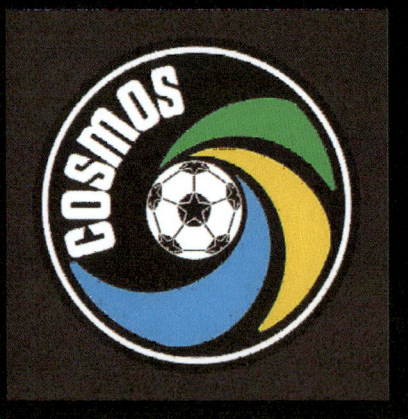

Carlos Alberto with the NY Cosmos in 1979

Hennes Weisweiler, Coach od NY Cosmos

Zamalek SC Crest

New York, 1980s

club's announcement of a thousand-pound insurance policy on his foot. A year later, he learned that he had played for ten months straight on an injury of which he was unaware: kidney muscle fibrosis. Ten months playing in the shadow of a torn cruciate ligament, or fever, or an ankle injury, and gallbladder removal. Two months later, his silent sit-in was considered playing hooky, and without any acknowledging of the matter he refused a transfer offer from the Emirati club Al-Ayan, which was accompanied by a fee of 25,000 pounds and a monthly salary of 3000.

Who made Farouk?

A year later, Farouk was serving the end of a new sentence for playing hooky, with a two-month suspension, which finished after 40 days. This whole period was permeated by a request for "forgiveness from the public," and "no one made me," "Zamalek deserves the main credit," "the desire to live a decent life," "Farouk makes greedy requests." He travelled by shuttle to Jeddah, Baghdad, Kuwait, and London before returning to Cairo, where customs charged him 40% of the cost of a car worth 19,000 pounds, a gift from a Saudi prince. Business included 50 imported watches and a sandwich shop, all symptoms of the era that Farouk collected very early, in which the word "future" formed the common denominator of his speech.

Hello…How are things at home?

The traditional morning call home contained disturbing news about the illness, and monotonous news about Zamalek not missing him in the next match against Factory 36. During a massage session near the Dumbo neighborhood in Brooklyn, Farouk tried to ignore the news bulletins, which tracked the progress of negotiations to free the hostages at the US Embassy in Tehran. Still, he couldn't stop himself from remembering that he was stuck temporally and spatially, along with his Iranian Cosmos teammate, Andranik Eskandarian, who had not returned to his homeland since the revolution. The only difference being that Eskandarian—one of the stars of the Iranian back line at the 1978 World Cup—had a key role in the Cosmos line up, alongside Brazil's Carlos Alberto, while Farouk's place was still vacillating: between being one of the most important players on his continent during the second half of the seventies, and his status as an illegal immigrant on probation, his fate hanging on a Brazilian coach who was about to leave, and a German legend of the magnitude of Hennes Weisweiler. His savings were drained, and he still didn't know his official status as an amateur or professional player, about the bridges burned in Cairo, or a city whose moods it was tough to adapt to, as she tried, under the guidance of her new mayor Ed Koch, to recover from the recurring risk of bankruptcy.

Farouk surrendered to the steam bath, trying to rid himself of the slap he had received from his manager, Yakan Hussein, as punishment for not following instructions in 1974; the abuse from "General" Khalil al-Deeb, for expressing his desire for foreign professionalism; running behind the car of his favorite star Saleh Salim through the streets of Garden City; the 42 pounds rent on the apartment that he received as a gift from one of his fans in Zamalek; the first time he was unable to buy a gift for the first girl he fell in love with; the dust left by the first Volkswagen he bought in 1972; the ten pounds that he received as a reward; the words of Mohsen Hassan Hilmi, the club president, who'd said that Farouk was a "problem child."

An anti-Iranian protest in Washington, D.C., in 1979. The sign reads "Deport all Iranians" and "Get the hell out of my country" WikiCommons

Andranik Eskandarian WikiCommons

CAIRO

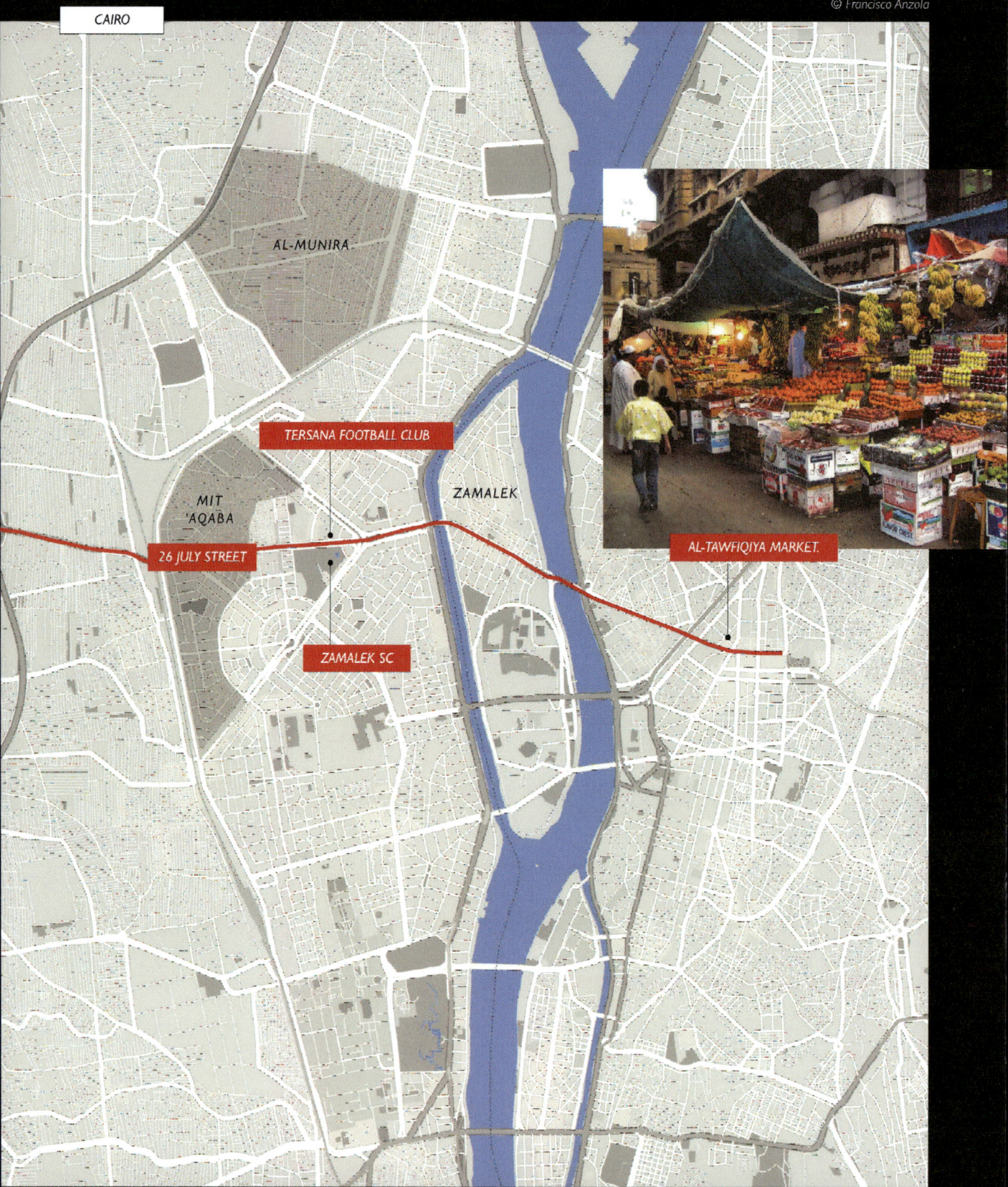

AL-MUNIRA

TERSANA FOOTBALL CLUB

MIT 'AQABA

ZAMALEK

26 JULY STREET

ZAMALEK SC

AL-TAWFIQIYA MARKET

© Francisco Anzola

Also: a table in a modest home bearing the remains of lunch for ten siblings; al-Munira close to sunset, after the end of the football matches with homemade sock-balls; the daily 147 bus journey to Mit 'Okba, which might include a free ride if the conductor recognized him; his fear of drowning at sea; the flight information screen in Rome airport on September 26; the looks of his comrades in the national team when he told them he was heading to New York, along with the girl he was seeing, who subsequently became known as his wife. The short conversation with Mohammed Jaber "Nour al-Sharif" in the Zamalek under-18 team, and the savings book from which Hassan Hilmi used to give his players their allowance. The *fatir* bakeries on 26 July Street in the mid-sixties (two piasters for a pie) and his first monthly salary of 30 pounds. The flaming stands of the Cairo stadium in '71 after the clashes with Marwan Kanafani, that ancient wooden shop belonging to Uncle Mujahid at the Tersana football club that specialized in customizing sports shoes for players (for seven pounds), and riding behind Ghanem Sultan on his motorcycle, going to his fruit shop in al-Tawfiqiya market.

Tersana SC Crest

Lost hopes

The agreement that Farouk pursued with Cosmos was that he was seeking half a million pounds for himself and a million for Zamalek, his "first home," waiting for the determination of his legal status as a still-amateur player, which might not guarantee the club any rights, especially as the US Soccer Federation, the federation for professional footballers, was not yet registered with FIFA, the international federation. The subway journey from Queens to Brooklyn forced him to contemplate the graffiti, and the gangs of youths flooding Manhattan, who had become heroes in the film *The Warriors*. As he passed through the East Village, Farouk didn't pay much attention to the frenzy surrounding Debbie Harry and the pop group Blondie; he wouldn't be able to recognize David Byrne from Talking Heads hovering near Park Avenue, or accompany Joey Ramone on his failed attempts to ride the icy waves at Coney Island, or walk at night among the nightspots near Sixth Avenue or Paradise, with the rich and famous of the day in Studio 54 near Broadway, or the new paradise for the toilers at the Paradise Garage near Hudson Square, or one of the strongholds of the new gay community in New York, full of danger near Hell's Kitchen, and the girls of the night around Times Square, all during a year which ended with the assassination of John Lennon in front of his house.

Besieged by prejudice

Between watching Soul Train on weekend mornings, and nights in the company of the TV series *Mork and Mindy*, Farouk was like an alien who had landed at the wrong time, forming part of a major cultural experiment begun by the Cosmos team ten years earlier, in an attempt to integrate the game of soccer into the city's already busy schedule, along with the New York Yankees, the Mets, the Jets, the Rangers, and the Knicks, representing baseball, hockey, American football, and basketball, the quartet of professional leagues around which Americans' minds revolved throughout the year. Farouk was the second African piece, added on to Abdul Razak al-Ghani, who had established his presence there before going to the Arab contractors years later in a great farewell.

Karim Abdul Razak Tanko playing for Cosmos nasljerseys.com

Stamp for the Mediterranean Games in Split
(Yugoslavia then) 1979

Al-Ahly SC crest from 1952 till 2007

Zizou (Abdel Aziz Abdel Shafy) playing for Al-Ahly

Hassam Helmi (President of Zamalek SC) playing tables with Sadat; www.filgoal.com

Before resolving to continue his adventure with Cosmos, Farouk first needed to resolve all the dichotomies that constantly pursued him: amateur/professional, father/son (with Hassan Helmi), personal dream/first house, the future/public adoration, riches/sacrifice, independence/security. These were the dichotomies that formed the raw material for the cases of mutual extortion of Egyptian footballers in the early seventies, as one of the first sectors to adopt the trend of the new reality of the post-October period, bearing in mind that the Al-Ahly administrators had always marketed paper as some kind of moral superiority, and there was always that player who rejected an offer, preferring to remain with the crowd, supporting his players, unless the administration saw that the player's interest required them to go through the experience in order to enrich Egyptian football!

Farouk's decision to emigrate, made at Rome airport, on his way home from Split, appears consistent with the new reality that Egyptian football was experiencing at that time, with around ten players travelling or rather "escaping" from their clubs directly to clubs in the Gulf states, in pursuit of tempting contracts, which above all were fixed. Farouk was no more than the most famous hero of the situation, amidst the continual calls from a large contingent of players for the contracting process to be legally codified, connected to a specified time period, and, in return for a fee, include health insurance. There were also calls for an end to the practice of bartering players' futures against the issue of fame or national reputation, an issue that didn't have a purely local dimension. But the second half of the seventies was the most tumultuous period in terms of strikes and stoppages, and the formation of union-style organizations by large sectors of professional sport.

The cortisone generation

The matter appears even more urgent in the Egyptian context, overshadowed by the automatic treatment of football at that time as something decidedly trivial, yet unfortunately popular. Let alone taking into account Farouk's membership of the "cortisone generation": a whole group of players immersed in a sea of misdiagnoses and incomplete treatments, spending entire seasons under the influence of painkillers. The list of absences from the Egyptian national team between 1977 and 1982 is noteworthy, as is the number of players who suffered the penalty of early retirement. Suffice it to say that Farouk, along with Zizou, to date the youngest player to represent Egypt internationally, were on the verge of quitting the game altogether before turning thirty, and this because of injuries suffered over several years.

The real irony was that Farouk moved from an Egyptian economic context, which imposed a new reality that rejected him for his social insignificance, despite his popularity with the crowds, to a new economic reality that seemed very serious, where he was searching for a fanbase from scratch. Farouk spent the first half of his life battling his amateur status, playing 88 international matches at different age levels (university, club, first team, youth team, the military), without by the age of 28 establishing a rational base, like the Eastern European systems, to allow him to gain experience. Then his future was taken hostage by his amateur status during the second half of his life, as he began the eternal journey of return, which has long inspired Egyptian football in general, and Zamalek especially. This is the return journey of the prodigal son, the path of forgiveness, the journey of absolution, the tearful return of Essam Bahij to his big house in the movie *Hadith al-Medina*, followed by Shehata Abu Kaf, that dreamy duality between player and sin. Farouk decided to purify himself on the following March 17, talking to Hassan Hilmi about the decision to return, preparations for the popular reception at the airport, ethical disciplinary actions, the first appearance on the international

Shehata Abu Kaf

Essam Bahij played himself in the film "Hadith al-Madina" (1964), in which his level of play deteriorates after he meets a playful girl. This affects his future, so his teammates and friends cooperate in pressuring him to leave the girl and go back to how he was.

1979 COSMOS   Won 24, Lost 6

Front Row, Left to Right: Johan Neeskens, Wim Rijsbergen, Vladislav Bogicevic, Giorgio Chinaglia, Technical Director Prof. Julio Mazzei, Captain Werner Roth, Coach Ray Klivecka, Franz Beckenbauer, Dennis Tueart, Carlos Alberto, Eskandarian.
Middle Row, Left to Right: Head Trainer Joel Rosenstein, Hubert Birkenmeier, David Brcic, Terry Garbett, Nelsi Morais, Marinho, Goalkeeper Coach Miguel de Lima, Santiago Formoso, Seninho, Mark Liveric, Eric Delabar, Erol Yasin, Assistant Trainer Arnold Trachtenberg.
Back Row, Left to Right: Equipment Manager Charlie Kessel, Ricky Davis, Gary Etherington, Godfrey Ingram, Antonio Carbognani, Boris Bandov, Kevin Eagan, Joe Filian, Jeff Durgan, Greg Ryan, Abdul Razak, Ron Atanasio, Assistant Equipment Manager Bob Russo.

Lobby

Skating at Rockefeller Center, ca. 1980, Library of Congress

club program, explaining the situation to the "public," supporting Zamalek to win the club championship, which had been lost the previous season and was at stake this season.

Farouk finished his habitual visit to the Rockefeller Center, which was in those days the Cosmos club headquarters, hoping to test his legal and material position. The idea of remaining still obsessed him, as he cast hazy glances at the Soviet-style mural in the lobby and then the famous ice rink attached to the building. This was all part of his big dream. Farouk knew the seventies well—he could read them amazingly well, but it was a premature reading. He had to wait until the advent of the nineties to be technically free to manage 18 clubs over a quarter of a century, beside hundreds of sessions of television "analysis," a way to combine financial return and image, alongside a lot of sarcasm that did no harm at all, for the self-parody that had tainted the progress of that generation over the previous three decades became an important source of income. Farouk discovered his mother tongue early, the same language that made Egyptian football such an important cash cow for the company Presentation, which made the domestic league in its current form resemble a luxurious aquarium, which was only permitted to be viewed from afar, a collection of colorful fish circulating through plastic grottos; nevertheless, everyone ate their cake from it, without ever achieving the goal that Farouk and his generation strove for, which was creating a truly professional career path, since the Egyptian league remains one of only a handful of league championships in the world (including the Somali, Eritrean, and Ethiopian leagues) not recognized as a professional tournament according to FIFA regulations, missing more than one deadline to bring this about.

Return from Cosmos

The walk across Union Square and alongside Central Park was Farouk's favorite part, as he escorted his friend from the Egyptian Consulate. He was completely unaware how extraordinary that period of New York life was, in one of its most lonely and anarchic periods, in the midst of a fuel crisis, which became a source of nostalgia over the next 35 years, especially in light of the prices currently being chased by the real estate market. Farouk could only hope to surpass what his compatriot Osama Khalil had achieved at the Philadelphia Fury. As his return to Cairo in March drew closer, Pink Floyd's album *The Wall* pervaded Queens. Without a single official match for Cosmos, without the half-million announced, all of Farouk's thoughts were on the possibility of catching the Mansoura match in May (he later scored two goals in it). At the end of the year, he was sentenced to 15 days in prison and three pounds bail in the case of assaulting Jamil al-Maghazi, the Al-Masry team doctor, during the match between the two clubs in the 1980–81 season. Everything returned to normal. For many years, he tried to remember the name of that song that always accompanied him during practice days that first January, about the girl who posed a question to Robert Holmes in the classified ads, "If you like Pina Coladas, and getting caught in the rain, if you're not into yoga, if you have half a brain, … call me." Robert Holmes was the only one who answered the call.

Farouk as a coach

Italy

The Roof

By **Najwa bin Shatwan**

Translated by
Nariman Youssef

By night, Andrea Giordano was the security guard at his hometown's town hall, and by day, a goalkeeper for the local football team. When he took off with his teammates for the San Paolo tournament, unknown burglars took advantage of his absence and pinched the town hall's roof.

Although the townspeople wasted no time in rushing to the mayor's house to inform him of the robbery, it took him a while to grasp that his office was, in fact, missing a roof and that, from now on, he would be known as the Mayor of the Town Hall That Had Its Roof Stolen. Half-dressed, he rushed out, the townspeople in tow—on foot and on wheels—embellishing the story of the robbery all the way to the center of town.

The mayor was shocked at the state of his office. Overhead, storks soared toward the lake. A nest had toppled off the edge of a wall, leaving a mess of broken eggs all over the floor. The mayor's thunderous shout made the building's ribs shudder: "Damn you, Andrea! Damn you, Andrea!"

He immediately penned an order to fire Andrea and slapped him with a hefty fine, then stood wiping the sweat and bird droppings off his bald head. "Damn you, Andrea, and damn your mother and father!"

Andrea retaliated against the town by joining the rival town's football team as a reserve goalkeeper. This rekindled an age-old resentment between the two towns that took on hellish dimensions when the rival team decided to change tactics and add Andrea into its next formation. Andrea took the opportunity to smash the ball into his former town's net, scoring a shock goal that left both sides gaping.

To put an end to Andrea's attack on their town, the burglars returned the town hall's roof, along with an envelope containing the total fine that had been levied against Andrea.

Meanwhile, behind closed doors, a delegation from the town was negotiating with Andrea over his price for the opponent's net.

Within a year, Andrea's life was completely transformed, not because of his lofty ambitions, but because a new roof of sturdy concrete had been raised onto the town hall, which now also boasted newly installed steel locks on its doors and windows. Yet none of this could stand in the way of Andrea, who knew that the way to penetrate the town hall's defenses was to keep the palms of the staff well-greased.

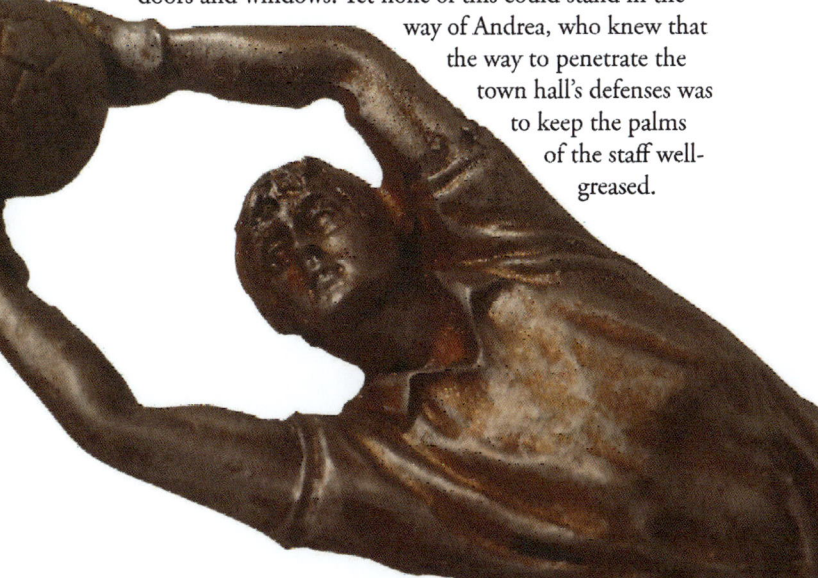

Iraq

The Cloven Ball

By **Yasmeen Hanoosh**

Translated by
Leonie Rau

On his tenth birthday, Salam received a new football. It landed in his arms suddenly, as if it had fallen from the sky. Despite his stubborn questions, no one seemed to want to tell him where the ball had come from. In time, he accepted it as a miracle. So often, he had dreamt the dream that all his friends shared: that he had a real football all to himself, to replace the dirty rags he and his comrades had collected and formed into a round shape so they could at least play with the illusion of a ball, if not with the ball itself—a ball that would make him popular and adored among all the neighborhood's children. They would run after him barefoot, begging him to let them play with it. He would make up strict terms for this and that; he would dictate that the game take place in the dust of the old cemetery's square, what the rules of the match would be, who would be on which team, and so on.

Salam's great wish came true. Not only was the ball the only foreign product that entered his working-class neighborhood during the time of the fatal embargo, and the highest-quality football ever made—it was the kind you just kick and it scores goals and guarantees victory after victory for its team—it was also a magical ball of exceptional appearance. The design on its skin was unique: While most footballs possess geometric hexagonal or abstract shapes, the design on this particular ball was in a map of the globe with all its cities split in half. Its rivers and plains, mountains and seas, and all other topographical features surrounding those cities had also been split, such that the known world with all its geographical characteristics appeared divided into two halves on the surface of the imported football.

However Salam looked at this ball, at whatever hour of the day and from whichever angle he wished—as he usually did in his bed in the morning before dribbling it to school, or in the evening when he was stretched out on his mattress after the satisfying exertion of a match—it always appeared to him that the football's world was cloven in two. Two parallel, equal halves in every respect, which were at the same time in utter disagreement.

Salam also noticed that the ball was inhabited by creatures, tiny people that were hardly visible to the naked eye, with loud voices that sounded like human ones, or sometimes more high-pitched than humans.

Over time, it became clear to him that the ball's small and relatively dimwitted inhabitants all believed in some kind of amusing superstition, the general notion being that every soul was created round—in the shape of the globe they lived on—before being split, with half of a soul placed in each body. Each of them had to wait to meet their soul's other half on the other side of its divided land, after all the cloven parts were reunified. Salam also observed that the entire population of the two hemispheres was obsessed with colors. Each half had a color that set it apart from the other. According to the inhabitants, it was this color that distinguished them and made them stand out from the other half. For example, if he were to listen to the inhabitants on one half for a while, he would hear them claim that their color was the only true color in life, whereas all the other colors were an abhorrent error. And when Salam listened to their clamoring in the silence of the night, trying to work out each side's convictions on various topics, he would hear them say that their food was the healthiest, their clothes the most elegant, and their conduct in life the noblest and most civilized.

If the matter had been limited to a difference of opinions and the preferred colors of the peoples of the two sides, it wouldn't have been so very strange. However, the most astonishing thing about the dispute was that it usually revolved around matters on which the two sides' opinions coincided entirely: the blue side, for instance, was always criticizing the red side for its method of child-rearing. At the same time, their own people were raising their children in the same environment of violence, division, bullying, and vengeance—without even realizing it.

In the beginning, Salam thought that a fever had struck him, making him see these things happening on the ball, or that he was hallucinating for some mysterious reason, and so he tried to ignore these scenes and suppress his feelings about them. In time, though, he realized that the events happening on the ball had become visible to all his friends, since they had become increasingly reluctant to participate in the cemetery matches.

The most severe misfortune to strike the children of the neighborhood, however, was a reflection of the deadly and regular attacks each side of the ball began to launch against its counterpart. Each side claimed that the other belonged to them and that they should form an indivisible whole together. Despite both sides agreeing on this goal of unity and their shared history in the daytime, they still attacked each other at night. This usually followed a dispute over control of the borders, chipping away at those same foundations, with one side announcing that the other was violating the conditions of the ancient agreement and the idea of inevitable, if tarnished, unity.

Whenever one of the children kicked the ball, they would hear one side say to the other: "Get it straight! Are you blind to what matters to this nation? Shame on you for believing in such nonsense!" Then they would go and believe in—or even preach—the same position, after scoring goals and winning matches.

Salam was sometimes woken at dawn, in those small hours that he no longer spent in the serene calm he had previously enjoyed, by the noise of the insults the two sides flung at one another.

After months of avoiding any interference in matters that didn't concern him, Salam thought of mediating some of the negotiations. He hoped that he could perhaps help the two sides reach a ceasefire, or a rational solution to a few of the central disputes that seemed not only basic, but trivial. This undertaking, however, failed, because the two sides' arguments overlapped and contradicted each other, and it was no longer possible to distinguish between the position of one side and the other.

As time passed, corruption gained the upper hand, eating away at the football's once smooth and shiny skin. As the two sides took turns imposing sharp divides at the borders to maintain the safety of their people, crevasses and abysses began to multiply. The situation escalated to such an extent that Salam woke from his sleep to find the flaccid ball swimming in a puddle of tears shed by its divided peoples. The affair went on like this for several months, during which it became impossible to enjoy the usual football matches. It was as if the disease of discord had spread slowly among the members of the two teams, reaching a point where they fought each other, kicking with their feet and punching and choking with their hands whenever they tried to gain control of the ball or deliver the coup de grâce.

On a rainy winter morning, after a sleepless night during which the cries of struggle and fighting rose from the surface of the ball, Salam jumped up from his bed and retraced a blood-red stream until he reached the source of the commotion. He stood for a long time, statue-like, staring at the cloven parts. Suddenly, and without prior warning to either himself or the fighting inhabitants, he gave the ball a mighty kick with his left foot that sent it flying through his bedroom window, crossing the house's front garden and passing over the high brick wall that his father had erected after the uprising broke out, and onto the streets of his Hayyaniyah neighborhood and the main roads of Basra that branched out with their accumulated rubbish. The ball was flung north over the Jabaish marshland and the Euphrates River until it arched west toward Najaf, continuing its journey along passages of stifling hot air. Over Iraq's western desert it made an astonishing leap, splashing a drizzle of contagious discord.

It passed over thirsty fields, tired villages, and the arid deserts around the region of al-Rutba, spreading an epidemic of disharmony onto the sparse green and abundant desiccation. It continued gliding through the air, its curse beginning to reproduce and multiply with each of the ball's rounds across the heart of the burning sky, until, finally, it landed in the lap of a new child, in another spot on its wretched map.

Palestine

Captain Majid

By **Ameer Hamad**

Translated by
M Lynx Qualey

My brother and I turned the shopping center into a football pitch, so that the minute our mother stepped into one of the stores, we would set off running and passing our little ball between us, slipping past the defenders with their shopping bags as we headed for the goal, which we had not yet spotted, but which we would find when a security guard would suddenly appear to take the ball away from us, and then we would score a beautiful goal between his feet, after which we would leap up and down in celebration, along with the mannequins in their glass cages.

Our friends called us the golden duo, because we played together in harmony, just like Majid and Yassin in the cartoons, and when we passed the ball, we could turn the players on the other team into shoppers whose hands were full of heavy bags.

We joined our city's club, and we rose up through the different age groups until finally we were in the last one, the one just before the first team.

The competition was ferocious among the players, and there were only two spots open on the first team. The distance between me and my brother Majid was growing larger, and my limited talent, plus my glassy body that was riddled with injuries, didn't allow me to stay in the golden duo as Yassin. My brother was promoted, and another player took my place alongside him. I ended my series of injuries by tearing my ACL, which led to a knee operation, after which I thought it better to stop playing.

In the first matches that my brother Majid played on the first team, he sat on the bench until the very end of the match, when the coach put him in along with Yassin. My brother's team was one goal behind, and so the golden duo started running and passing the ball between them, turning the stadium into a shopping center, and, when they reached the goal, Yassin passed the ball to Majid, and he put it between the goalkeeper's feet with a smooth touch, scoring the equalizer.

When I leapt for joy at the goal, my injury gave a painful throb. I sat back down, feeling—as I watched the golden duo celebrate—the scar from my operation, which had sunk its path deep into my knee, so that I was imprisoned, like a mannequin, inside my glass cage.

Palestine

Captain Rabeh

By **Ameer Hamad**

Translated by
M Lynx Qualey

The first ball he got as a child was stuffed with cotton and had a smiley face printed on it, and he didn't part with it, not even in bed.

In the hallway that connected the bedroom he shared with his younger brother to their parents' room, they—he and his brother—transported the Captain Rabeh cartoon from the television to their own stadium, where his ball transformed the two open doorways into poles, crossbars, and goal nets, and the throw rugs into soft grass that turned the feet green.

When he asked his ball which shot he should choose, in order to score a goal, she would answer—without stopping to smile, and after checking the goalkeeper's position—that he must perform a "missile" kick that turned into a tiger when it took off, or a "mirage" shot that disappeared between the goalkeeper's fingers, or an "Aquila shot" that soared like an Arab eagle into the sky, then descended to tear into the net.

Then it came time for him to apply his skills outside, when his father enrolled him at the nearby club so he would stop breaking things in the house.

The way the others looked at his small stature wasn't like his brother's admiring gaze. The goalkeeper was about the size of his father, wore gloves like a boxer, and his goal was surrounded by an iron net that didn't tear. The playing field was asphalt, pitted with potholes. The shoes pressed into his feet, pinching one of his toes. And the ball was inflated all the way up, like the tallest of mountains, her features faded from the long days of children tormenting her with their blows, so that only a silent frown remained.

Egypt

What If the Elephant Is the Room?

By **Muhammad El-Hajj**

In Muhammad El-Hajj's short story "What if the Elephant Is the Room?"—part of his upcoming short fiction collection Two Stories About Masculinity—the protagonist, Mahmoud, is obsessed with the thought that his wife, Doha, might be having fantasies about her ex-boyfriend, Wael Ragheb. In this excerpt, Mahmoud recalls aspects of his relationship with Wael, particularly their football games together, and how the field often became a site for contesting masculinities. Mahmoud met Doha through Wael, and—unconsciously, perhaps—the way he sees his wife's ex-lover on the field continues to color his perception of him, threatening his marriage and, eventually, his own sanity.

Translated by Yasmine Zohdi

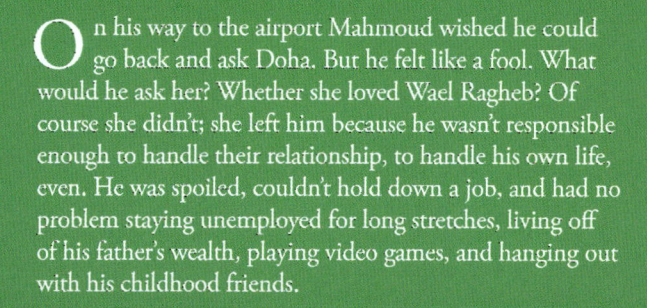

On his way to the airport Mahmoud wished he could go back and ask Doha. But he felt like a fool. What would he ask her? Whether she loved Wael Ragheb? Of course she didn't; she left him because he wasn't responsible enough to handle their relationship, to handle his own life, even. He was spoiled, couldn't hold down a job, and had no problem staying unemployed for long stretches, living off of his father's wealth, playing video games, and hanging out with his childhood friends.

He met her through him. Wael was not a friend of his, but he was among the group he played football with weekly. He used to play defense, trying to make the best possible use of his sub-par fitness level, while Wael was a striker. Wael was faster, more skillful, but he, too, was hard to tackle. He was a thorn in Wael's side whenever they played on opposing teams, even though Wael managed to get through him at times—truth be told, he'd lose the ball to him more often than he'd lose it to any other player. Once Wael was trying to pry the ball from his feet after he had just received a pass from one of the midfielders on his team. Mahmoud wasn't really a masterful player, but in that moment, something inspired him to pretend that he was just about to kick the ball, before gently nudging it in the opposite direction, smoothly bypassing Wael in the process. Somebody yelled: "He just killed you, dude!"—and the playing field instantly echoed with similar comments, all mocking Wael: "You're finished!" "Better sit out the next game!" A silent respect had dominated their interactions since then, and afterward Wael would always make sure—subtly, without any overt pronouncements—that they were on the same team.

Wael would sometimes bring Doha to the playground; she'd meet him there and they would go out after the game. That was how Mahmoud met her for the first time. She happened to sit next to his duffel bag twice in a row, and in the weeks that followed they would exchange shy nods to say hello, before they ran into each other at a wedding, in line for the buffet. He wouldn't see her for a while after, and when Wael invited him to his farewell party before he traveled to Spain for graduate school, Mahmoud noticed her absence and guessed that they had broken up. Months later, he met her again by chance, when her search for an interior designer who could fix up the office of the startup where she worked led her to his firm. He didn't get the job, but they stayed in constant touch while he was working on the pitch and throughout the long process of negotiations around the budget he presented. He appreciated her attempts at persuading her boss to choose him, and he didn't feel particularly bitter that he didn't get the job. To thank her—and for other reasons—he took her out to lunch one day. He didn't speak much; he spent most of the time watching her instead. At some point, she caught him gazing at her while she ate.

"Are you watching me?"
"Yes."
"Why?"
"I like you."

He had never been bold. In fact, he'd always been known for a particular kind of stability, which initially stemmed from his shyness and an ingrained fear of rejection. His only other serious relationship had begun after he'd spent almost two years harboring a secret crush on one of his friends, and even though she showed interest, it was never enough to encourage him to actually tell her, until one day she asked him, clearly, and he answered just as candidly. She was surprised at his ability to articulate his feelings—if that was the case, why had he never told her how he felt? She never got an answer; she never even asked. Like him, her conservative upbringing had instilled a fear of showing affection, even curiosity. Theirs was a brittle relationship, one that eventually snapped under the weight of her parents' financial demands once he proposed to her.

He had changed a lot in the three years he spent alone after they broke up. He kept a low profile and focused on building a successful career. When he wasn't working, he was either playing football or binge-watching American TV. When Doha appeared in his life, he was ready to commit.

He was feeling more comfortable with himself, a comfort that allowed him to let his thoughts simmer without fidgeting. Even the fact that he knew her ex-boyfriend—which previously would have prompted him to seek out more information about that relationship and whether she still had any feelings for him—didn't cause him much concern. He just told her how he felt, the moment he felt it. He had no bigger explanations.

During their trip to Morocco a year after their wedding, they were swimming in the natural pool at Akchour, gazing up at the waterfalls, when Doha told him that the thing that had attracted her to him the most, on that day he told her how he felt, was his confidence. He confessed then that he had been intimidated by her, and that if he had planned for it in advance, he probably wouldn't have gone through with it. Floating on her back in the deep green water, she told him that she wasn't really looking for a relationship back then, which bothered rather than flattered him. Then she turned to look at him and said that the moment he told her he liked her, she knew they were going to get married. He laughed at her statement, but she insisted that she knew. She asked him if he remembered her response, and he answered, mimicking her:

"You're not so bad yourself."

She laughed, and he laughed because he loved it when she laughed, and she swam toward him and they held each other tightly. It wasn't that long ago, that perfect moment—three, maybe four years. What the hell, then, brought them back to Wael Ragheb?

NEW BOOKS from
THE LIBRARY OF ARABIC LITERATURE

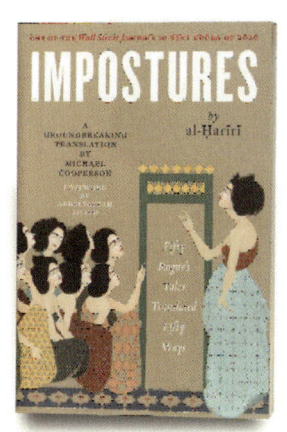

NEW IN PAPERBACK

"An important translation of a criminally neglected work of world literature."
—Mada Masr

Impostures
by al-Ḥarīrī
Translated by Michael Cooperson
Foreword by Abdelfattah Kilito

The adventures of the man who created Aladdin

The Book of Travels
by Ḥannā Diyāb
Edited by Johannes Stephan
Translated by Elias Muhanna
Foreword by Yasmine Seale
Afterword by Paulo Lemos Horta

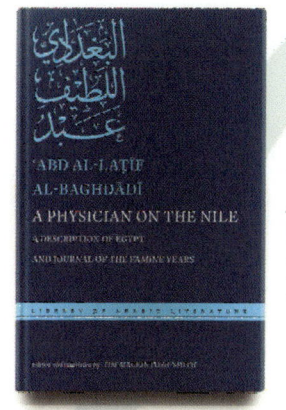

Flora, fauna, and famine in thirteenth-century Egypt

A Physician on the Nile
A Description of Egypt and Journal of the Famine Years
by ʿAbd al-Laṭīf al-Baghdādī
Edited and translated by Tim Mackintosh-Smith

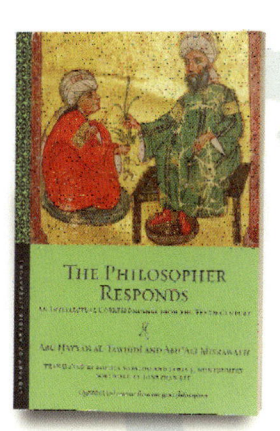

"A fascinating read, particularly for the aspiring scholar of classical Arabic texts."
—Al Jadid

The Philosopher Responds
An Intellectual Correspondence from the Tenth Century
by Abū Ḥayyān al-Tawḥīdī and Abū ʿAlī Miskawayh
Translated by Sophia Vasalou and James E. Montgomery
Foreword by Jonathan Rée

Available online or at your local bookstore
WWW.LIBRARYOFARABICLITERATURE.ORG
WWW.NYUPRESS.ORG
WWW.COMBINEDACADEMIC.CO.UK (UK/EUROPE)

Palestine

A Tin Ball

By **Adania Shibli**

Translator
anonymous

The war, it seemed, was over, after it had reached the far extremes of violence. In short, it had reached a peak, and here were the soldiers packing away their possessions and collecting their equipment, tired, exhausted, and spent, having given all their energy to battle. Therefore they went on tossing everything without much care, into their kit bags and vehicles. There were vehicles for carrying the troops, then others for carrying military equipment, for the crates of bullets and grenades, for transporting tanks, and for the tins of food, some past their expiry date. As far as the eye could see, these were the only things that had survived undamaged. Buildings all around, however, had been shelled and were now riddled with haphazard holes, lumps of them dropped onto the streets and pavements, and paint peeled from their facades and interior walls, which still surrounded the furniture that those fleeing the bombardment had been unable to carry with them. Less visible were the corpses of all ages scattered around the place. Or, maybe more accurately, they should remain invisible. Instead, focus should be limited to their numbers, and if there were enough time, it would be possible to mention their names and ages, then the circumstances of their deaths, including what they were doing at the instant they were killed, and what they would nevermore be able to do. Except this would be an arduous task. In fact, it would be nearly impossible to gather all this information, which would most likely be forgotten at the nearest available opportunity, regardless of the considerable amount of sympathy, even sadness, it may elicit. Nothing of the sort will be done here, though, eliminating the possibility of this text being read as political propaganda that may provoke the ire of certain readers, particularly those from the ranks of the intellectual middle class. Anyway, these bodies, if they mean anything to anyone, other than those to whom they belonged, it would be to those who were closest to them, and perhaps their killers as well. Not now, but later. Most likely, many years later, because now these killers are tired, exhausted, and spent, and are using whatever energy they still have to collect their possessions and their equipment, to leave this battlefield and get back to their homes without delay. So they must collect everything that has survived undamaged or hasn't been used, and put it either in their kit bags or in the appropriate vehicle. And everything that has not survived or has been used, they must collect into huge garbage bags, a task which they perform without the care they give to collecting their possessions and equipment. Nevertheless, when they leave the place at last, they will leave some of it behind, and not only the garbage bags. In the meantime, distant voices will be heard, claiming that love and peace will triumph in the end, and medical teams will get ready to enter the place, followed by the international press, humanitarian aid convoys, and human rights organizations, and slipping in behind them, a group of mischievous, curious children. As soon as they're in, each group will go on searching the place for anything that might fall within the scope of their interests. No need here to spend too long going over these interests, since they are well known. Therefore the text will turn directly to that group of mischievous, curious children which this time numbered among its ranks Mohammad, Mounira, Moneim, Mazen, Maysoon, Mukhles and Maya, all of whose names, by sheer coincidence, begin with the letter M. Apart from that, and although they were born to families with different economic and social backgrounds, they have one other, fundamental thing in common: poverty. Mounira was the eldest, but Mohammad was the strongest, and the pair led the group through the almost abandoned battlefield, with Maya, youngest and smallest, always at the rear.

Every age and size has its advantages and disadvantages, but Maya was currently experiencing the downside only. While other members of the group rifled the soldiers' refuse for wonderful, rare and valuable things, she was finding things that were plentiful and that nobody cared about, like empty sardine tins and bullet casings. She went on to collect them, tossing one away whenever she found another in better condition, keeping the shiniest and least battered, until, at last, she found a sardine tin with the lid only slightly peeled back, though it was totally empty. And Maya immediately began filling it with the little bullet casings she'd collected and kept. Slowly and carefully, she slotted them in one-by-one, until the tin was full of casings stacked widthwise, at right angles to the way the sardines are usually arranged. Then, all of a sudden, shouts of surprise and admiration came from the group up ahead, who then started running, with Maya following after though she had no idea why, except that in the current circumstances she, like them, was driven by an instinct to stick together always, as much as possible.

They all ran until they came to an area clear of buildings and people, where they used to play during peacetimes. Mounira sat down, and Mohammad followed suit, while the others stood clustered around them. As silence reigned, Mounira took a disc-shaped metal tin from beneath her shirt. There was writing on it, which none of them could decipher, though they knew exactly what it was from the image beneath it. An image of dull green cucumbers. Mounira began wrestling to open the tin, while Mohammad gave his instructions on how to do that, before he soon intervened, pulling the tin from her hands. Not that this meant that Mounira lost control of the tin. Not at all. Meanwhile, drool had started to build up in the clamped mouths, swallowed back whenever the dammed mass rose too high to breathe. They, for certain, did not think of themselves as extremely poor children, but tinned pickles were a rarity in their food basket or, for that matter, in the landscape of their daily lives. Sometimes they'd spot them in the refrigerators of newly married couples, or at a lunch or a dinner party. But to find them like this, while they were playing around, was unimaginable. The question now was how many pickles were in the tin, and the number that each would get. There must be at least seven in there. Ten, perhaps. And it would be acceptable by everybody that Mounira and Mohammad, who'd found the tin, got the biggest and the most once the rest of them had been evenly divided, with the smallest pickle going to Maya. Her body, being the smallest and the youngest, did not really need so many. These thoughts, inner wonderings and imaginings, continued to occupy the tiny heads until, at last, the tin broke open. At first a *ting*, the sound of its opening then grew into the rasp of tearing metal, as the reek of pickling juice reached their nostrils, growing sharper as the tin was passed between Mohammad and Mounira. It was a process not so much of passing the tin as of a reluctant parting, until it came to rest at last in Mohammad's hands, while Mounira went on taking out its contents. Pickle by pickle, they were distributed first to Maysoon, then to Mazen, then to Mukhles, then to Moneim, and, finally, to Maya. And truth be told, after much inspection and examination, there didn't seem to be that much difference in size. With Mohammad and Mounira keeping hold of the tin and whatever was left inside, everyone began to gobble down their share. And while most of them finished off their pickles, despite trying to eat as slowly as they could, Mohammad and Mounira did not. So murmured pleas started to be heard, begging a bite from one or the other, just a little one, and Mohammad and Mounira rebuking the pleaders, but even so, granting them the tiniest of bites, until the group had finished off every pickle in the tin and only the juice was left. So they started to drink that, each in their turn, and no one drinking more than everyone else, and if anyone did, as was the case with Moneim, then Mounira would snatch the tin away. Fairly, we said!

Afterwards, Maya excluded, they split up into two teams of three, and began punting the tin back and forth between them. And whenever the tin was kicked too far away, Maya, who was standing on the side too young and too small to know how to play football, would rush to fetch it.

It was a truly beautiful day that none of them would easily forget, ever. They were happy.

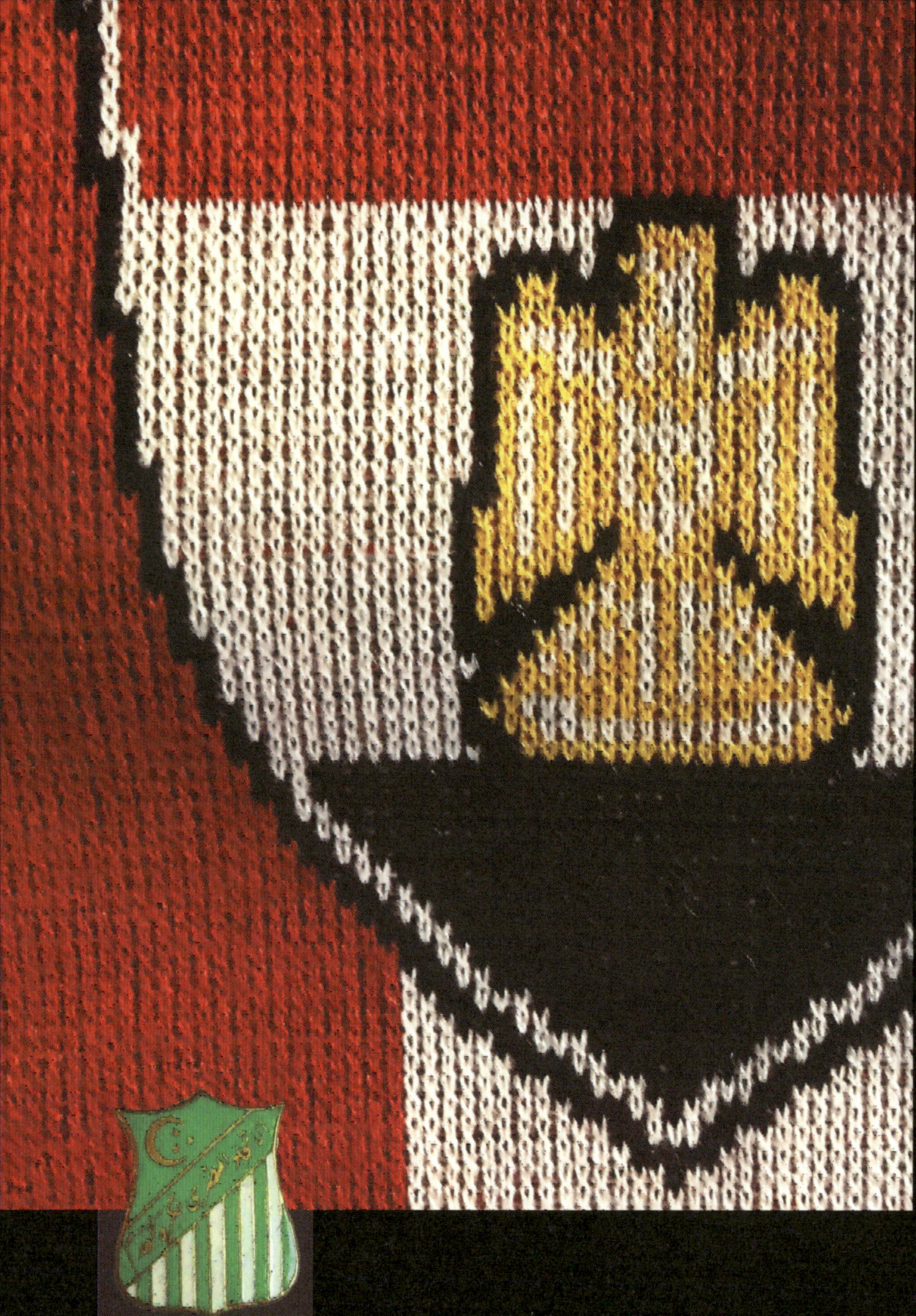

Gallery

Egyptian Football's Missing Archives

By **Mina Ibrahim**

CAIRO

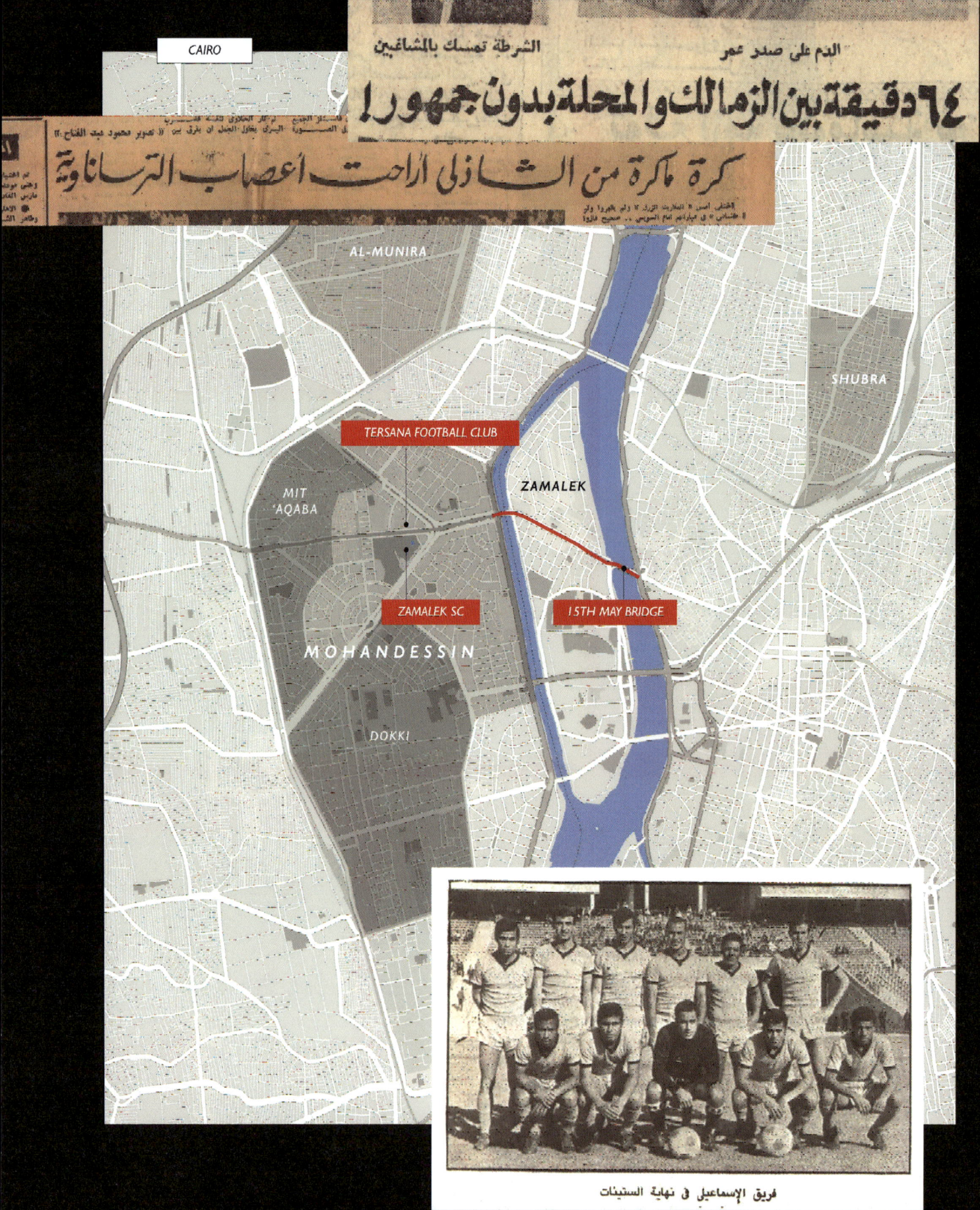

الدم على صدر عمر   الشرطة تمسك بالمشاغبين
٦٤ دقيقة بين الزمالك والمحلة بدون جمهور!

كرة ماكرة من الشاذلي أراحت أعصاب الترسانا

AL-MUNIRA

SHUBRA

TERSANA FOOTBALL CLUB

ZAMALEK

MIT 'AQABA

ZAMALEK SC   15TH MAY BRIDGE

MOHANDESSIN

DOKKI

فريق الإسماعيلي في نهاية الستينات

I don't remember the first time I went to a football stadium in Egypt, nor whether it was with my friends or my older cousins. But I can recall the day I chose to go alone. It was in December 2009, and I was two months from turning 18. It was a cold Saturday evening in Mohandiseen, which is in the Giza governorate of Greater Cairo. I had just finished a private lesson at an educational center close to Sudan Street. As every week, I had to cross the 15th of May Bridge to get to Dokki, in order to pick up a microbus and get back to my neighborhood—Shubra. On this particular Saturday, I had to go to my neighborhood parish to attend a Coptic prayer called *tasbehat sab'a w arba'a*, which takes place during the Coptic month of *Kiahk*, in the four weeks that precede Eastern Christmas.

I didn't have much experience with Mohandiseen, even though Shubra is not far off. I walked along Ahmed Orabi Street until I reached the fence of al-Tersana Sporting Club. The lights of its small stadium, and the queues waiting in front of its gates, drove me to ask about the day's game. My excitement increased when I learned that al-Masry FC, from the coastal city of Port Said, was coming to play against al-Tersana SC, which is based in the area of Mit 'Okba in Mohandeseen. By placing this memory into the context of Egyptian football history, I came to an important conclusion:

We must have a popular archive to hold our shared memories of Egyptian football.

Neighborhoods

For this classic game between two teams, both established at the beginning of the 1920s, al-Tersana SC and al-Masry FC were wearing their home jerseys, blue and white respectively. They are both labeled as *'andiyya sha'biyya* (popular clubs, or clubs that have fans). This term appeared in the early 2000s, when a number of companies and state institutions in Egypt began to have football teams playing in the Egyptian Premier League. During the 2020-21 football season, the league included a team presented by a petroleum company (Enppi), a team for the National Bank of Egypt (al-Bank al-Ahly), and another from the ceramics industry (Ceramica Cleopatra). This is in addition to two teams called The Military Vanguards and Military Production. Now, more than a decade after the game I attended in 2009, Tersana SC has completely disappeared from the first division of the Egyptian League. The club where Hassan el-Shazly—the league's all-time top scorer—once played can no longer compete with the aforementioned clubs, nor with others recently founded by Egyptian and Arab businessmen that do not have any supporters such as el-Gouna FC, Pyramids FC, and Wadi Degla.

Today, it is rare to find a neighborhood football club playing in the first division of the Egyptian league. We can have a club connected to a city such as Mahalla Textiles, which, although it holds the name of a factory, is beloved by many who live in the city of Mahalla. Moreover, there are the two most famous clubs, al-Ahly and Zamalek, whose supporters can be found across the country, but also among other Arabs. Unfortunately, with the privatization and capitalization of football in Egypt, there is a serious concern that the Egyptian league might turn into a so-called *dawry sharikat*, or a league of companies. Much like the neighborhood clubs, supporters of al-Ittihad al-Sakandry of Alexandria, al-Masry of Port Said, and al-Ismaili of Ismailia City told me that they are afraid their teams might lose their presence in the Egyptian Premier League.

Tersana SC crest

Al-Masry FC crest

Egyptian Football Association crest till 1958

Egyptian Football Association

Alexandria Stadium; the first in Africa and the Middle East

Parade Générale Le jour de l'Inauguration du STADE 1929

Celebrational stamp for Egypt participating at world cup 1990 in Italy

Coin toss between Turkey and Egypt before the Summer Olympics match on 28 May 1928.

Gaafar Waly, The first president of both the Egyptian Football Association and Al Ahly sports club at the same time

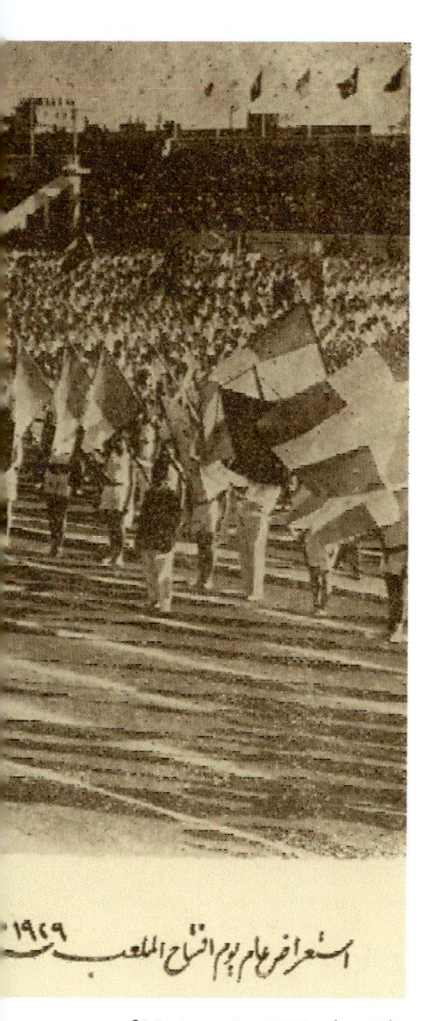

The fans are alarmed by the upcoming 2021-22 football season, which witnessed the promotion of three teams: Coca-Cola FC, Pharco FC, and al-Sharkiyya Lel Dokhan. A fan of al-Ittihad Assakandry told me, "The first is a beverage company, the second produces medicines, and the third is for cigarettes and hookah flavors…now the cigarettes and the cola bottles that used to entertain us while we watched the game, and the medicines that we used to take when our teams make us sick, are now playing with us…"

Martyrs

When I went to the stadium of al-Tersana in December 2009, I was not a supporter of either team. But I had to join the fans of the home team, al-Tersana SC. I had no other choice, since the fans of al-Masry FC usually arrive together from Port Said in organized groups. I asked about the price of the ticket, and it was three Egyptian pounds, which, at the time, was less than one US dollar. At this point, I had to sacrifice some of my money for the game and thus would need to walk for longer to get a cheaper microbus to Shubra. "First come, first served" was the rule in Egyptian stadiums at the time, until a company called *tazkarti* computerized and monopolized the selling of tickets when Egypt hosted the 2019 African Cup of Nations. In 2009, the tickets for any game didn't specify your seat, and neither did the cement benches where we were seated. The tickets just had the logos of the two teams and the Egyptian Football Association (EFA), together with the game's time and the date.

I loved the coincidence that allowed me to share this moment with the inhabitants of Mit 'Okba, who had a team close to their households, schools, workshops, and stores. I remembered what I had read and heard about the ESCO club in Shubra, and how al-Ahly and Zamalek used to visit and play against this team in the '80s. ESCO was a member of the Premier League, and people used to call it and its stadium *bo'bo'* (the ghost of) the big teams. Now Shubra doesn't have a team to represent the daily lives of the people of Shubra, since ESCO was relegated to the second and later to the third divisions. Even those who do not support ESCO, but instead al-Ahly and Zamalek, no longer have a chance to see their favorite players a few meters away from their homes. They have to travel for long distances to one of the stadiums recently built in Egypt's deserts, such as Borg al-Arab and June 30th, which is also known as The Air Defense Stadium.

The game between al-Tersana and al-Masry was the first and last time I went to a stadium alone. As it is for many Egyptian football fans of my generation, a trip to a stadium is accompanied by traumas and nightmares. Even before Covid-19, the

Mohamed Farouk in front of ESCO Club at the start of his football career referring to the name of the club he played for at the beginning of his football career at the age of fifteen before moving to Al-Ahly.

Mohamed Farouk is one of the most prominent stars of the Red Castle in the late nineties until the beginning of the 2000s. With Al-Ahly, he won a number of titles during his career.

الأهرام الرياضي

CLUB WORLD CUP
ULSAN.H
TIGER UANL

هجوووووم

حمامة من الوصول الى الكرة قبل رجب   ((تصوير : رضا مصطفى

يتعادل مع الاسماعيلي ١/١

الترسانة "تشوى" كابوريا !

Egyptian Premier League had been missing its fans, ever since the 2012 massacre at Port Said stadium, when 72 al-Ahly fans died following a game between al-Ahly and al-Masry FC. Tragically, after the fans were allowed to get back to their seats in February 2015, the martyrs of al-Ahly were soon joined by 20 more martyrs, killed during a game between Zamalek and Enppi. On this day—February 8, 2015—a couple of my friends decided to buy tickets for the game to support Zamalek. They missed the smell of the green grass and the sound of the chants sung by tens of thousands. They prepared their shirts and white flags and drove to the June 30th stadium. A few meters away from the gates, they noticed the smoke rising from tear-gas bombs, and they heard the sound of lead bullets coming from beside the gates. That was when I decided that I would never go to a stadium on my own again. "I should be accompanied by a friend or a relative, so if I die, I could find someone next to me," I wrote in my diary.

The massacre at Port Said stadium

Missing archives

The day of the game is a special one, especially if you plan to go to the stadium. Unlike prominent European leagues, football games in Egypt do not necessarily take place on the weekend. So you may need to adjust your schedule based on the timetable set by the Egyptian Football Association. The latter is never consistent and can change at any moment, depending on security concerns or other unknown reasons. The absurdity continued when I randomly tried to find any video or mementos from the game between al-Tersana and al-Masry. "2009!" laughed an employee at al-Tersana SC. "This is too old…I don't think we have anything about this game."

What remains from the game is its final result: 2-1 in al-Tersana's favor, in addition to my fragmented memories. There is not a single photo or a ticket I could get from the abandoned archives of al-Tersana club or the Egyptian Football Association. I even lost my ticket—I did not expect that, one day, I would write down my witness of this game.

ENPPI SC crest

The game between Tersana SC and al-Masry FC in 2009 was on fire. The coach of the al-Masry team was Hossam Hassan, one of the greatest Egyptian football players. During the last years of his career as a player, Hassan had joined al-Tersana, after spending many years with al-Ahly and a few with Zamalek and al-Masry. Before the game, the fans of al-Tersana chanted for Hossam Hassan and his twin and assistant Ibrahim Hassan. But when the game started, and al-Tersana scored a goal, al-Tersana's fans began to insult the brothers. They insulted the president and the players of al-Masry. After the game, I remember that Hossam Hassan refused to respond to the fans of al-Tersana during the press conference, saying that he cherished the good memories that they had forgotten.

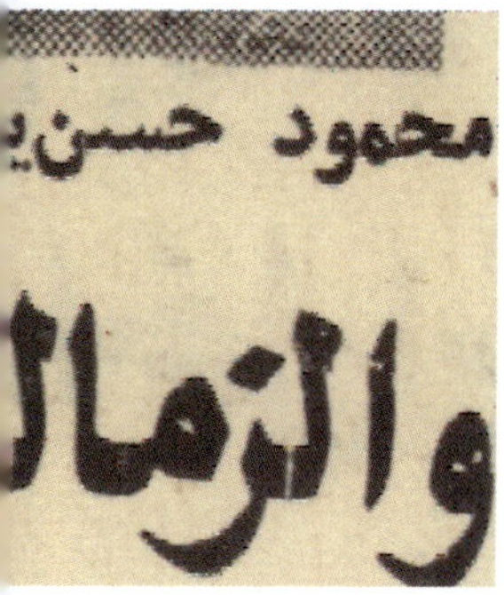

Insults are an essential component of the dynamics of football all over the world. During the game, al-Masry fans also insulted Mohamed Aboutrika, who was a player for al-Tersana before joining al-Ahly in 2004. In response, fans of al-Tersana who also supported al-Ahly boomed out their attacks against the team from Port Said. However, unlike what the mainstream Egyptian media has suggested, insulting the players of other teams—or even of one's own—did not start with the youth who founded the al-Ahly and Zamalek Ultras in 2007. Locating insults in the generation born in the '80s and '90s not only produces a naïve moral image of the past, but also reflects the absence of people-oriented archives about Egyptian football, which leaves space for undocumented nostalgia and ahistorical myths.

روز اليوسف

السيدات ولعب كرة القدم

منذ سنوات قليلة أنشأ بعض السيدات ناديا للتنس .

وقد بلغنا أخيراً أن بعض زعيمات النهضة النسائية يفكرن في تكوين فرقة للعب كرة القدم وأخرى للمصارعة والملاكمة وشد الحبل !!!

مطبعة بول باريه — حارة قايد نزهة ٨ بمصر

Street Tournament in Port Said, undated
Twitter @MohsenSaleh

المحلة تلحق أول هزيمة بالزمالك - الأفضل أداء - بهدف مفاجئ للناشئ طارق محجوب

تحكيم متمكن لبلال ، سيطرة وفرص ضائعة للزمالك ، بسالة نادرة للمحلة

المحلة — عباس لبيب

ابراهيم يوسف يطير فرحا بعد احرازه هدف الفوز على المجر
((تصوير : محمود عبد الفتاح))

Memorial edition of Al-Ahly shirt
Photo: M Lynx Qualey

Newspaper clips are from Kora Zaman Facebook account

Insults should be part of these proposed archives. More importantly, the archives must also include the experiences of the fans before, during, and after they come to the stadiums. On the centenary of the establishment of the Egyptian Football Association (which was launched in December 1921), we must create visual and audible archives of the fans' stories inside the stadiums. By assembling this tangible and intangible heritage, which reflects what connects Egyptian football fans to the games—such as match tickets, memorial photos taken during matches, public chants, insults, and feelings at the times of defeat and victory—we can restore Egyptian football to its missing fans and to the disappearing popular clubs. This project will be an ongoing, interactive dialogue based on oral history and ethnographic fieldwork. This piece is a pilot project by an early career researcher and lover of football, who insists on the importance of documenting people's lives through their passions.

Excerpt

Altun Kupri, Iraq
© Levi Meir Clancy; Unsplash

Football Games & Casual Gunfire

By **Iraqi Shalash**

The translated blog post here appears in the book *Shalash, the Iraqi, goes West!* translated by Zeena Faulk, which appeared as an ebook in the summer of 2021. The blog posts of "Iraqi Shalash" originally emerged online between 2005 and 2006, during the post-war insurgency in Iraq. Shalash took advantage of a technology that was new to Iraq, the Internet, to lampoon religious authorities, political corruption, the effects of the Iraq War, and economic injustice, all in a satirical and over-the-top comic tone.

Translated by
Zeena Faulk

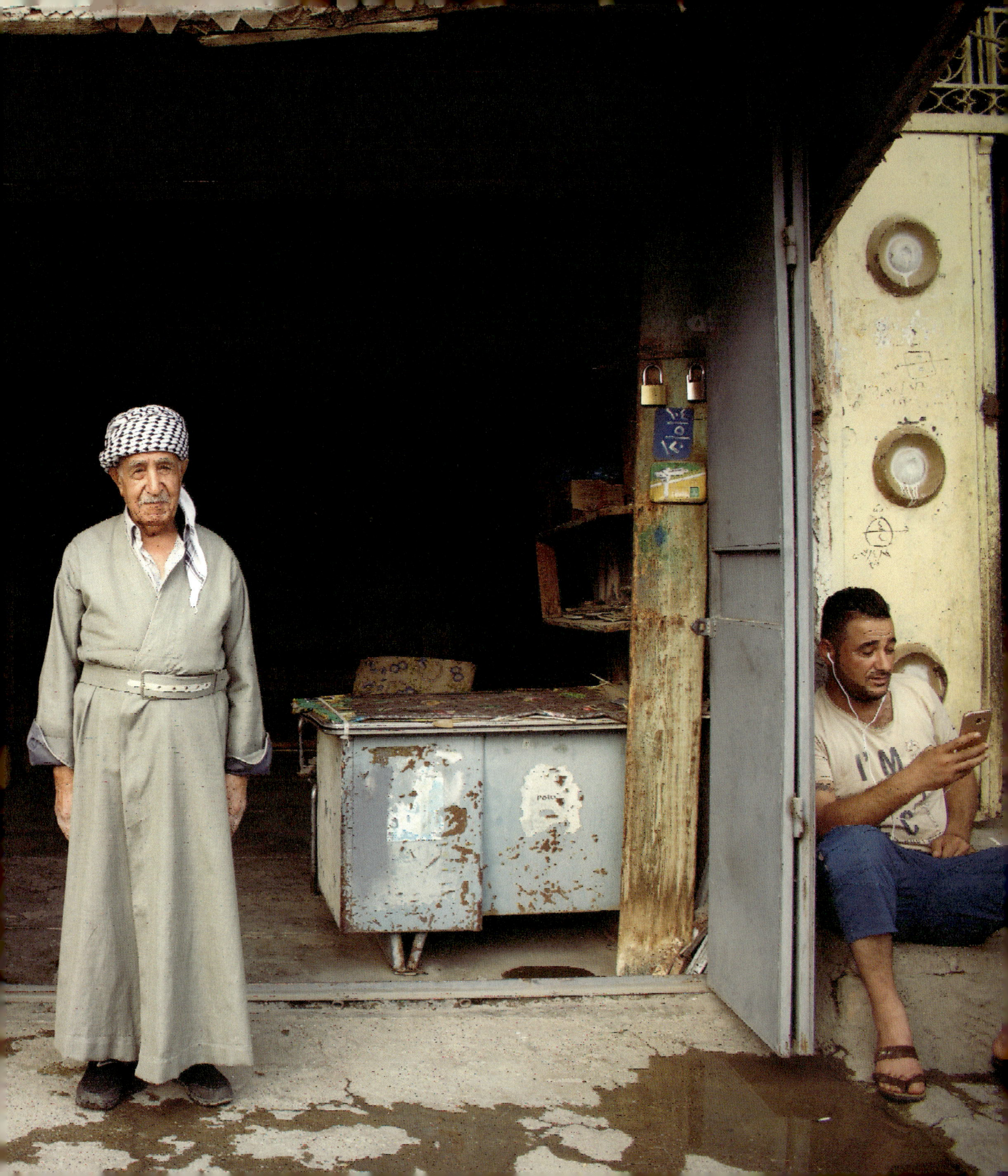

Have you seen how our football team is playing today? So far, our goalkeeper—Noor Sabri—has saved two penalty kicks and missed only one!

That's how things *should* be done. His performance brought me joy when I was really, really down. So I've decided to take a minute to share my feelings with you.

Sabri is indeed a virtuous man. Er, oops, I might have said that too soon. I forgot to ask around to see if he's Shia or Sunni! Duh! I'm entitled to ask, since I wasted twenty years of my life as a fan of Ahmed Radhi, Iraq's former football-team captain, who turned out to be Sunni. Radhi thought his Sunni faith qualified him to sit across from those candidates whose only qualifications were the foppish hats they wore in the Iraqi parliament.

Not only did he maneuver well in the green rectangle of the football pitch, but he was also skilled in Iraq's Sunni Death Triangle. What a pity! I remember how I often skipped school so I could breathlessly cheer Radhi as he ran through Baghdad's Al-Sha'ab Stadium. Oh gosh, listen to me go on! Sunnis are our brethren too, after all.

Don't you agree that the footballers' photographs are more beautiful than the ones displayed everywhere around our block these days?

The photos I'm referring to are ugly and frightening. Isn't that so? Our own children now refuse to go outside. And I don't blame them, for these frightening photos are right outside our doorsteps—and they go all the way to the street corner, the bus stops, and are even on television.

Photographs photographs everywhere, and yet no good face to see! It is as though the sky rains down these dreadful photographs, which makes me think about how much paper is being used. Wait a second, if we have enough paper to print these photos, why are our children still getting outdated school textbooks? Anyone with any decency would use the paper to print out new school materials rather than making more horrible photos.

Aside from these photographs, have you seen the signs everywhere? The material used to make these signboards, I bet my sweet ass, is enough to make undies for all the residents of Sadr City for more than ten years. And the slogans they're selling us have that cheesy, sleazy language:

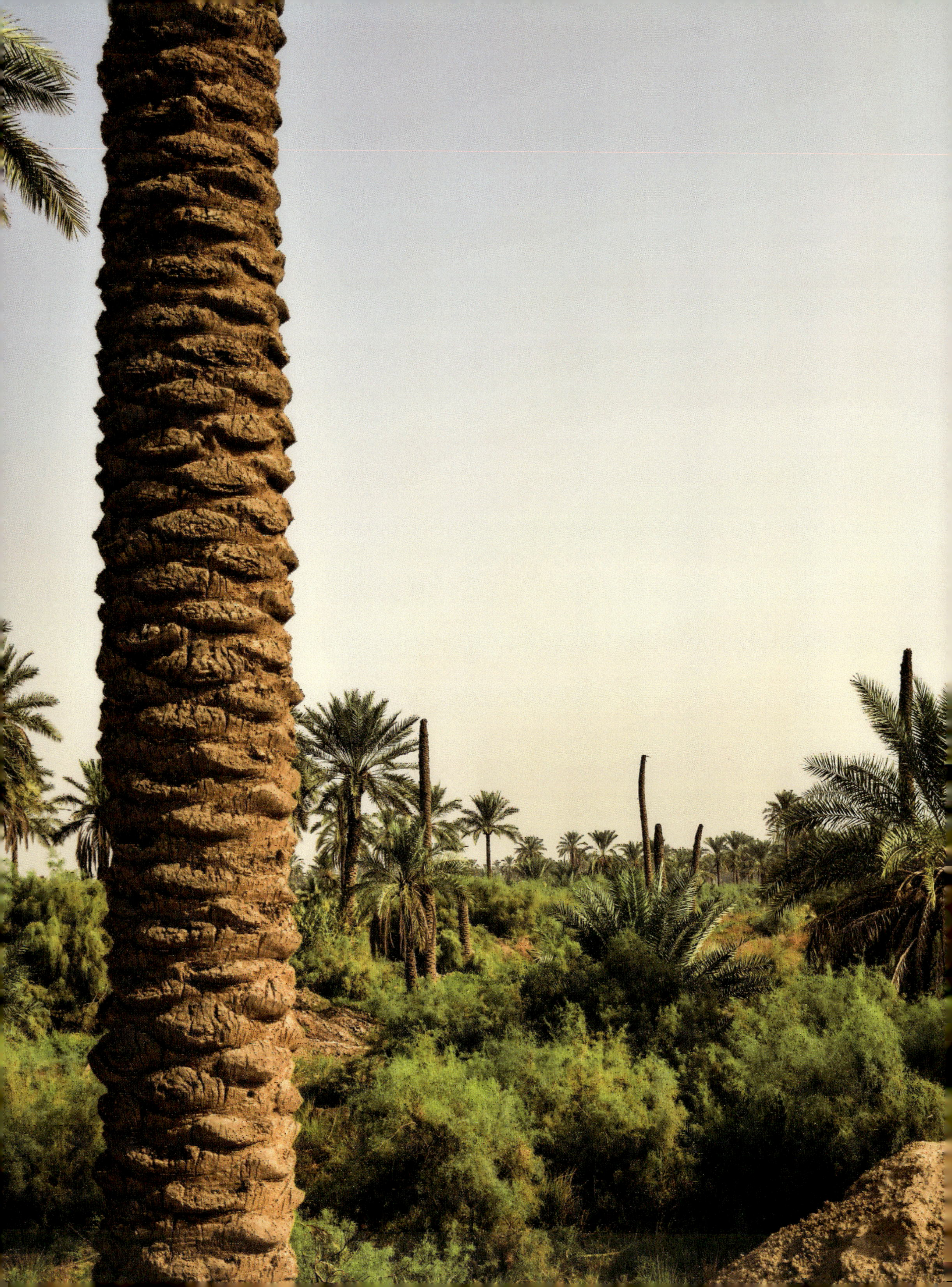

Baghdad, Iraq
© Abbas Almutta, Unsplash

Vote for the honest and strong man.
Vote for the stocky, baldheaded lad.
Vote for the man who was trodden by flip-flops.
Vote for the man who wasn't needed before.
Vote for the garbageman.
Vote for Jasimiyah.
Vote for the wobbly shower-mouth man.
Vote for the Iraqi sonofabitch who's the heroic protector of the homeland.
Vote for the blessed man and the son of the blessed.
Vote for the celibate and the son of the celibate.
Vote for the champion of the deprived and the victims' advocate.
Vote for the advocate of the poor.
Vote for the one who fights for women's rights.
Vote for the man who caught Saddam crouching in his hole.
Vote for the man who took on the cleansing of Sunnis from Al-Jadriya.
Vote for the man who fixed the electricity and water pipe problems, lied,
and played the poor people in this country who were starved
by Saddam for forty years and were fed mottos instead.

It is the same thing, folks, happening all over again with these newly arrived politicians, who are still selling mere words to the poor Iraqis. One politician assassinates the other in the name of democracy, which by the way should go to hell. We don't want it. Democracy doesn't suit us, and it is impossible to force it on people when all they've known is tanks on the streets and televised statements by the president.

Who the fuck would open up their mouth to say anything? We all ducked back into our houses like mice. We grew up knowing that we had only one "hero," and he beat the shit out of us. There are now a thousand heroes, all of them trained by you-know-who. New heroes advocating for democracy, yet no one can say a word.

Enough with the serious talk! Let's go back to football and focus on Sabri from the Iraqi team. My nerves were wrecked from the beginning of the game, and they stayed that way almost to the end. They were shattered, not because of the performances by the players who, by the way, did their best. I was on edge because of Eli, my neighbor's teenaged boy.

Two hours before the match, Eli took out his rifle and opened fire into the air. He was still shooting after the first match ended. After the other team scored a goal, he went on shooting, as if he were on the frontlines of a battlefield. I got so frustrated with him that I finally went outside to ask.

"Eli, what's going on? I don't get why you're shooting."

"What the hell? Is gunfire banned now, too? Man, I'm just expressing my happiness," he snapped back in a frustrated tone.

"Yeah, yeah! I get it. But most people shoot for a while and then go inside to watch the game."

"I won't stop shooting until the break of day tomorrow," he said defiantly.

"Why? Is the football coach your dad or something?"

"Go inside and don't philosophize with me. Let us express our feelings."

I was at a loss for words and ideas, but I did want him to stop. Suddenly an ingenious thought rushed into my head.

"Eli," I began, thinking quickly, "I heard that the Mahdi Army are coming into the neighborhood."

"I wouldn't stop even if the entire Mahdi Army came over!" he said confidently. "I'm friends with all of them, and half of them are family."

Eli, of course, was still firing as he answered. Coincidently, his father arrived, and that was when I offered up a silent prayer. I thought he would stop Eli, since he was a devout man and would not accept such behavior. His father slapped Eli across the face, took his rifle away, and started shooting himself.

1 Goran Street, Sulaymaniyah,
© Dastan Khdir; Unsplash

People, as I write this blog to post to you, the *righteous* father is still shooting. You know what? Maybe I should just post what I've written thus far, leave you to read it, and go outside to fire my gun as well.

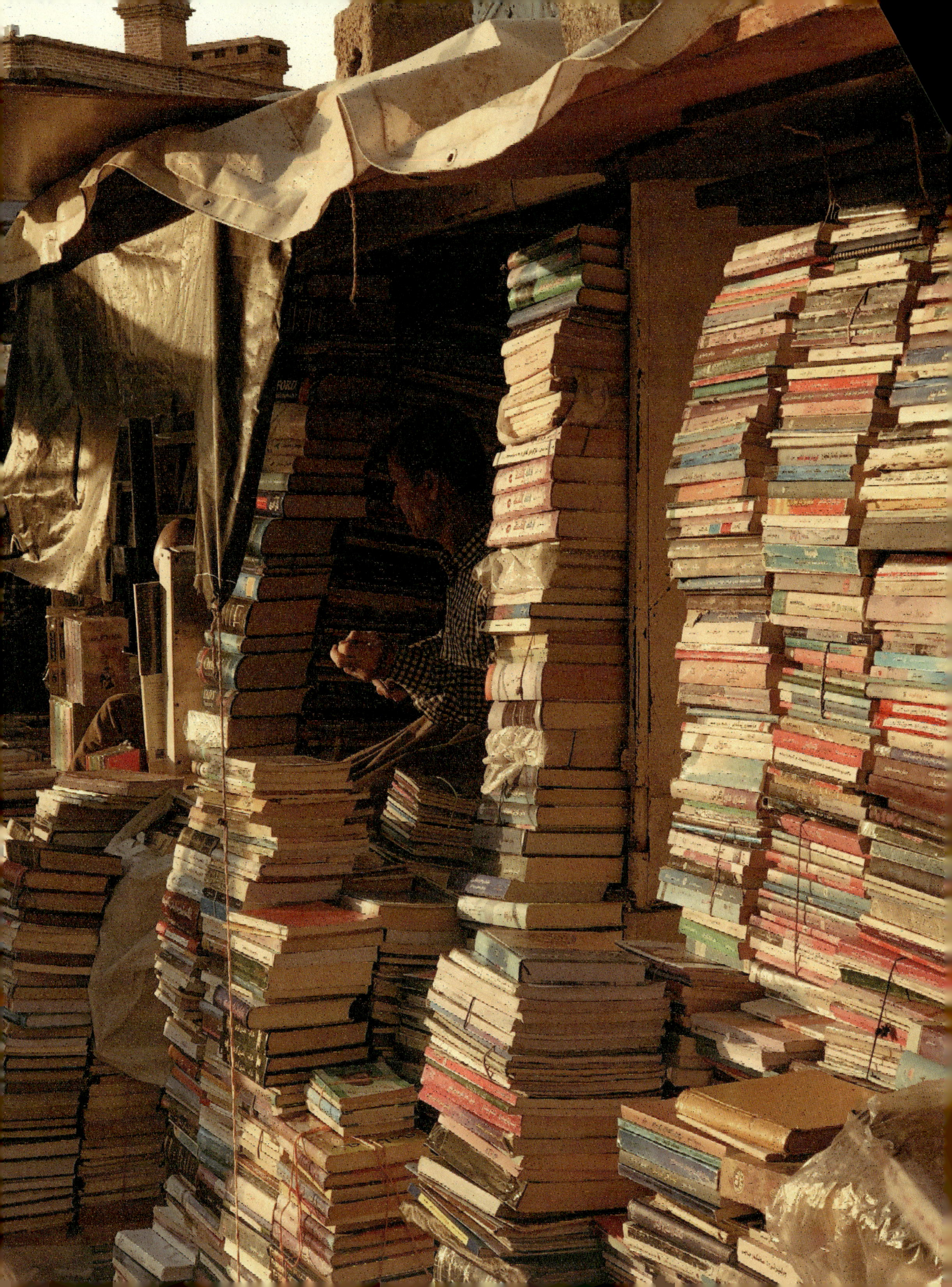

#TranslateThis

Diaries of a Running Man

By **Farid Abdel Azim**

Farid Abdel Azim takes the sport of football and uses its suspense, pace, and quick turns to create a narrative that, to the reader, feels like a football match. The story follows a young man's dream of becoming a footballer, and the daily struggles he faces with his father and life inside a totalitarian regime, en route to fulfilling his dream. The "running man" of the title alludes to all those who chase after success; the book was selected by the 2020 "Arab Voices" jury as a literary football novel-to-translate.

Translated by
Omar Ibrahim

From Chapter One

Continuous running causes sweating and panting, and it may also squeeze your heart.
There may sometimes be a sparkle of light that looms over the horizon, but it will soon disappear into the darkness. And if you ever venture to chase it, you'll feel as if you're searching for a needle in a haystack.

The road is long, painful and full of traps, thorns, and daggers.

I stood below that sparkle of light until it washed me inside out. I was tempted by the applause of the spectators. I found my dream between others' legs. I ran after my ball and passed it once, and then I received it and seized the perfect chance to shoot.

I shot it spontaneously, like a desperate suspect who has just been proven innocent. I shot it and shot my bad luck off with it. AND I SCORED! Spectators cheered, and they carried me on their shoulders, marching counter-clockwise around the field. It was as if we were performing the hajj rites. I was only half-conscious.

My lucky day came out of the blue, and all of a sudden I was their crowned king.

Every time I look back on my life, I become more and more certain that whatever is not related to luck is necessarily unreliable. The world's forces of evil gather for absolutely no reason except to prevent you from reaching your goal. They stand in front of you like a high wall to block your ball. Then, when you decide to drop your sword like a defeated knight, the wall is suddenly demolished.

That's what always happens before you declare your defeat: life smiles at you, coldly.

Then you glimpse a hole in the wall, through which your ball passes and shocks you by hitting the net. At that moment, you turn from a nothing to a hero, from a loser to an icon.

That's how I, Abd El-Maaboud Salah Abd El-Maaboud, changed from a tailor to Coach Abouda, the star who everyone admires in the old club.

Alberto Giacometti,
L'Homme qui marche I
Photo: Ania Mendrek

Excerpt

Mahfouz's Armband

From **Raja' al-Naqqash's**
*Naguib Mahfouz: Pages from his Memoirs and
a New Perspective on his Life and Work*

Translated by
Mahmoud Mostafa

Police Academy football team, Cairo, ca. 1930
© Private Collection

"Maybe no one would believe that, once, I'd been a football captain. My love for football lasted almost ten years while I was in elementary and then high school. Nothing could take me from football but literature, and if I had kept on playing, perhaps I would have been one of football's shining stars.

"My relationship with football dates back to the time when we moved to Abbasiya. At the time, I had just joined the elementary school, and my brother took me one day to visit one of his close friends from the el-Dewaney family, which was a reputable family, among the ranks of which were doctors and judges. The friend's house overlooked a railway station and, when we finished lunch, he suggested that he take us to watch a football match between an Egyptian team and an English one. Imagine my surprise when the Egyptian team won! Until then, I had thought that the English were invincible, even in sports. I went home that day obsessed with football and the names of the Egyptian players who had defeated the Englishmen, especially the team's captain, Hussein Hegazy, who was at the time Egyptian football's undisputed star.

"I asked my father to buy me a ball, and I insisted until he agreed. I started spending long periods in the yard outside our house, playing alone and trying to recreate what I had seen in this match that so captured my imagination, and very quickly I managed to master the basics. I joined El-Timple, or the junior team in elementary school. At the time, there was no age limit for admission, so you could find alongside the eight- and nine-year-olds young men in their twenties with big mustaches—hence the junior and senior teams. One of the senior team players was Mamdouh Mokhtar, who was also a first-team player with al-Ahly club; he was also a member of the Sakr family, from which Yahia and Abdel-Karim Sakr became famous footballers. With El-Timple, I played in the forward line as left winger, despite the fact that my left foot was non-dominant. This position limited my mobility, but nonetheless I was the team's top scorer.

"When I joined Fouad I high school, my position changed, and I became a center half. I excelled in the new position so much that a lot of people who watched me predicted that I would shine in football and would join one of the big clubs and participate in the Olympics with the national team; that is why my colleagues were astonished when I refused to join the university football team and, since then, my ties with playing football were cut. It was the same with watching the game after Hussein Hegazy retired.

The Graphic, February 21st 1925 A British weekly illustrated newspaper

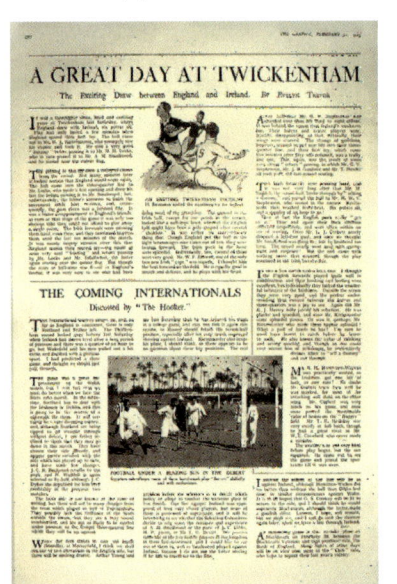

The caption reads "Football under a blazing sun in the desert. Egyptian schoolboys, many of them barefooted, play "Soccer" skillfully and with enthusiasm.

All players on the picture wear shoes though.

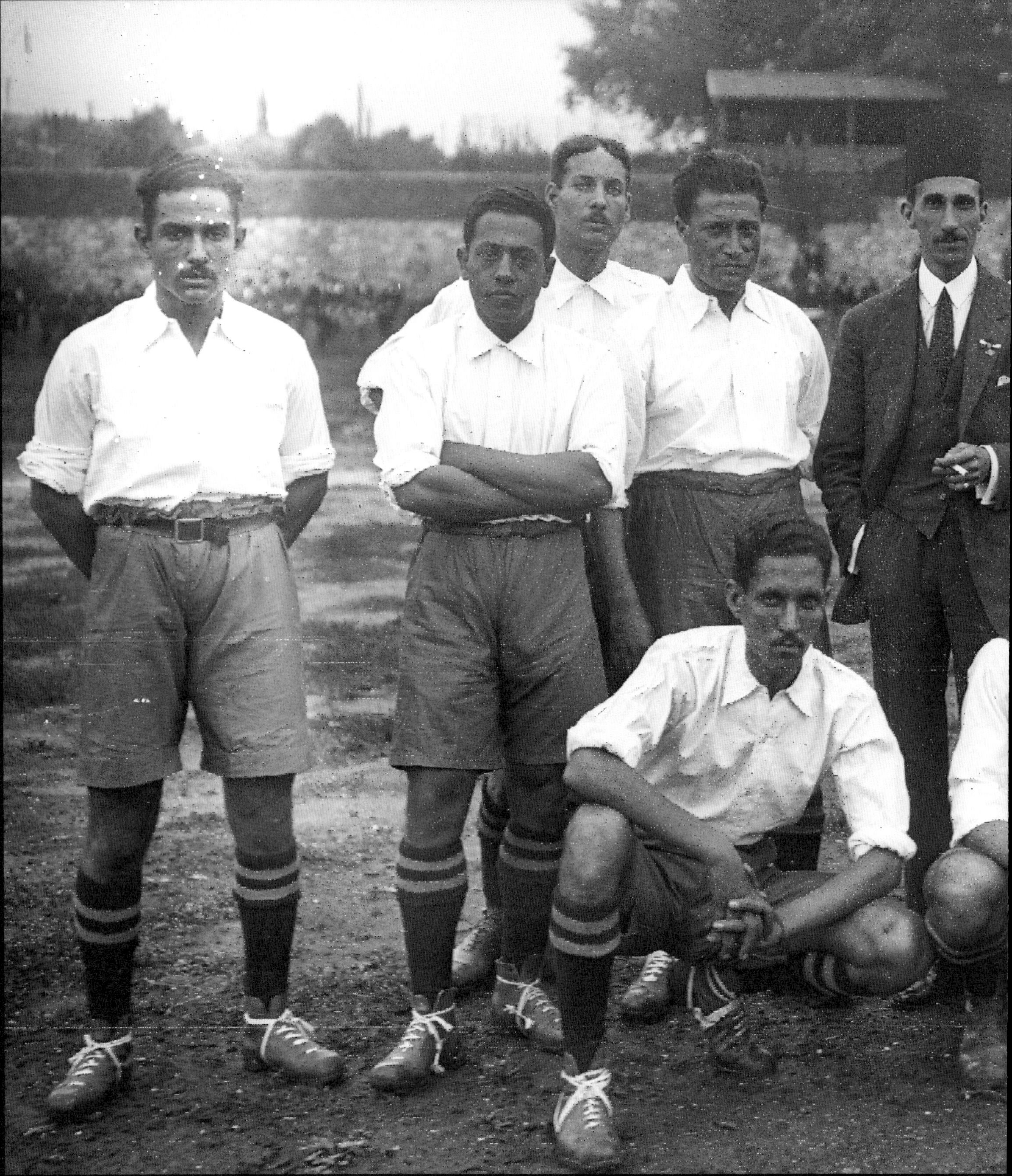

Egyptian national team, 1920

"For me, Hussein Hegzy was both the reality I could see and the myth that I had heard. I watched him in his dying football days, just before his retirement, and because of his unbelievable popularity and rare talent he continued playing to just shy of forty, which is an advanced age for footballers, most of whom retire in their early thirties. Despite his age, Hussein Hegazy held a presence on the pitch and, in the times I saw him, he showed characteristics that I admired, such as playing the role of maestro for his team and being a clean player, as he never intentionally fouled an opponent. He also had a powerful shot that allowed him to frequently score from the center line.

"This was what I saw of him; what I have heard was closer to legends that I couldn't verify, since some of it happened in England and some was in a period when I didn't watch him. It was said that his father sent him to England on a student mission. There, football took him from his studies, and he excelled at football to such an extent that they selected him for the English team, and he became one of the stars the press talked about, and they even changed the rules especially for him, so he could be the team's captain. It was said that the King of Spain attended a crucial match between Spain and England and was impressed by Hussein Hegazy and made sure to shake his hand after the match and told him, 'I wish that you were a Spaniard so you could play for us.'

"Hegazy went back to Egypt and became a member of the national team and participated in the 1928 Olympics, when the Egyptian team ranked fourth, if I remember correctly. Hegazy was the star of that team, and he received praise from the European press along with the Salem brothers, Mohamed and Ahmed. I remember that Mr. Wolf, our English teacher in high school, brought the *Times* newspaper to class and read aloud what had been written about the Egyptian team in the Olympics.

PAGE 84

"Along with Hegazy, another famous footballer of the era was Ali al-Hasany, who was a bully from Bulaq who played in central defense and had a strong physique and was notorious for his aggressive style of play. However, Mar'i the goalkeeper was even more aggressive, as his slogan was 'only the dead shall pass.' Mar'i was like a giant who can stop the ball with a single hand and handle it like a small orange. In *Mirrors*, I mentioned al-Hasany and, after the novel was published, I received a call from him, thanking me for remembering him. His voice was faint, and I learned that he had become bedridden and that sickness had worn him down. I was bewildered by the state of this giant of a man.

Hegazy (see arrow) with the Millwall Reserves team, in autumn 1912

Hegazy with the first Ahly team

Hegazy with the London FA team in 1911

شارع حسين حجازي
HOSSAIN HEGAZI ST.

Street sign in El-Sayeda Zainab, Cairo

رئيس فرقة الاعاهد ۱۹۲٦ رئيس فرقة تركيا

حسين حجازي نهاد عازم

Besides these players, there were: Gamil al-Zobair, Sayed Abaza, Mahmoud Mokhtar el-Tetsh, Mamdouh Mokhtar, and Mohamed Soliman, whom we called Hindenburg.

"While Hussein Hegazy was the captain of the Egyptian team, I wore the armband for the Lionhart team which I formed while in elementary school with my friends in el-Abaseya where the neighborhood streets were our home stadium. We used to host teams from other neighborhoods for fierce matches and go out to face them in their streets.

"After I was taken up with literature and overcome by reading and writing, I didn't continue watching and following the new generations and didn't know of any of them other than Abdel-Karim Sakr who emerged years after the retirement of Hegazy and was, as my friend Abdel-Moniem al-Shueikh asserted, a magnificent player with an unforeseen talent in Egyptian football. I don't know any of the current crop either. I remember that a journalist once arranged for a meeting between me and Mahmoud el-Khatib who was at that time a phenomenon, I couldn't tell him that I stopped watching football and that my ties were cut with the retirement of Hegazy.

"Sometimes, when I turn on the TV, I find a football match, so I watch and get nostalgic, and when the World Cup is on, I'll watch a match without knowing any of the teams. I started to notice that footballers have become wealthier than movie stars, when in the past a footballer's income was so miniscule that al-Hasany couldn't pay for his medicine after retirement. Footballers used to play as a hobby while having another profession to earn a living. Only the elites were able to dedicate themselves to football, as Hegazy was, because his father was an upper-class landowner. I remember that while working for the Ministry of Endowments, I met a young man who introduced himself as the son of Hussein Hegazy. I ardently shook his hand and said, 'Let me hug you. I clapped for your father so hard that my palms wore out!'"

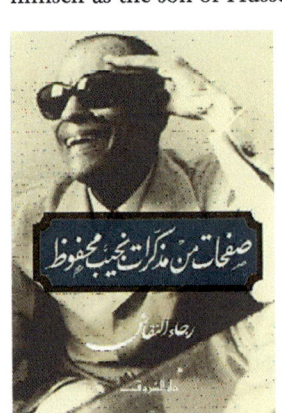

Raja' al-Naqqash, *Naguib Mahfouz: Pages from his Memoirs and a New Perspective on his Life and Work.* Cairo: Al-Ahram Center for Translation and Publishing, 1989.

Abdel Karim Sakr (1921 - 1994) of Egypt and Knud Lundberg (1920 - 2002, left) of Denmark shake hands before a first round football match at Selhurst Park football ground, London, during the Olympic Games, 31st July 1948. Denmark won the match 3-1.

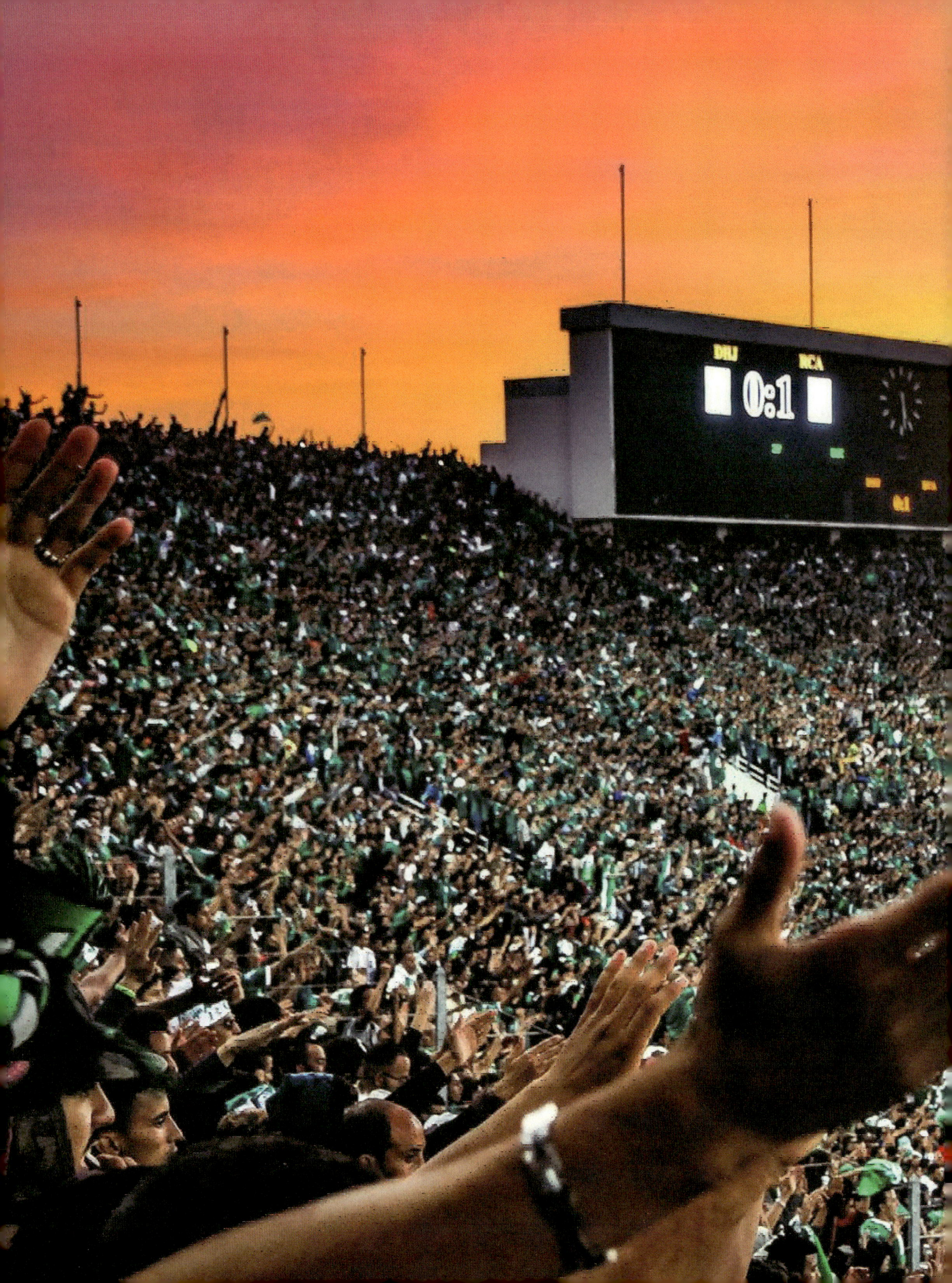
0:1

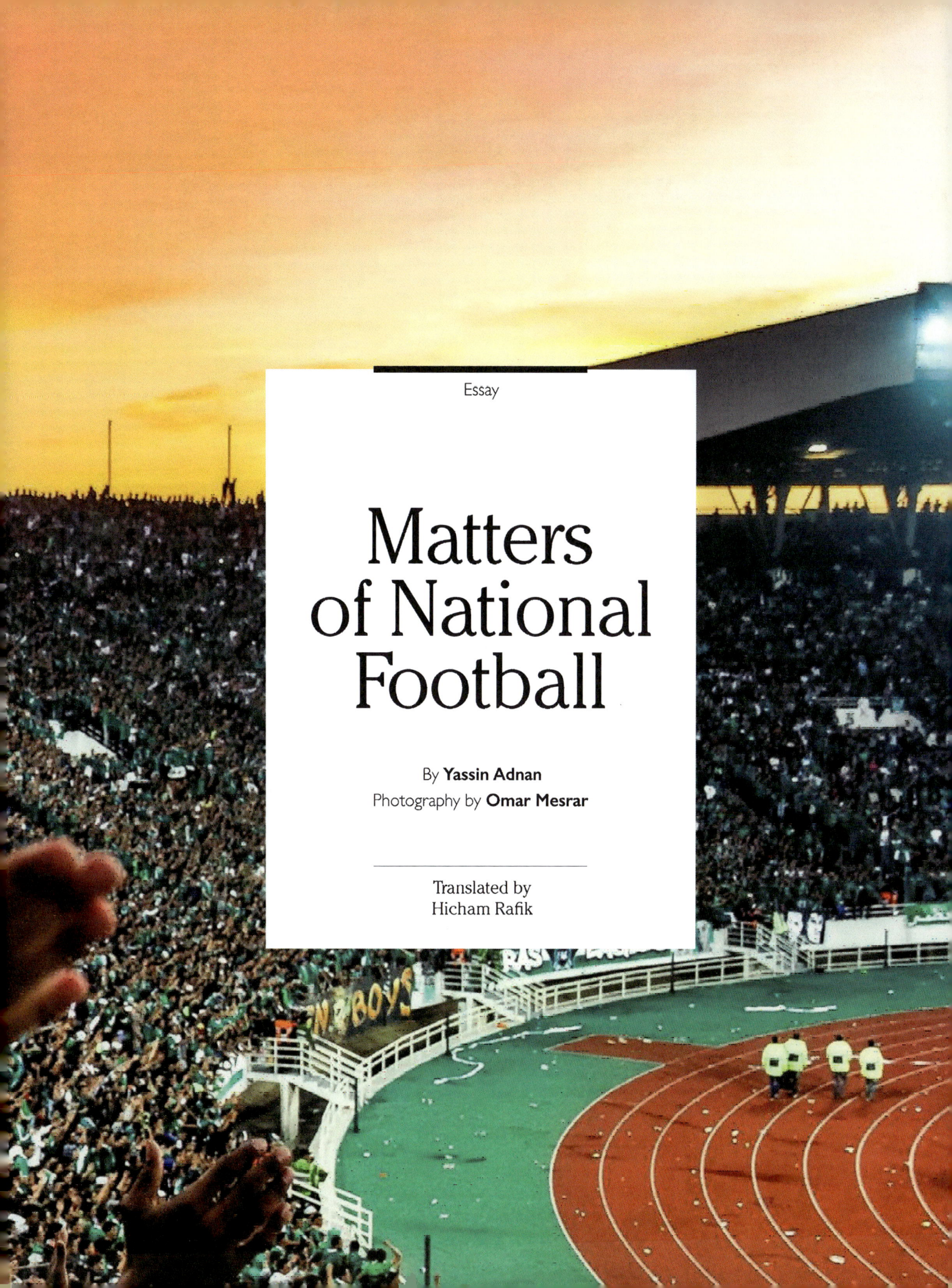

Essay

Matters of National Football

By **Yassin Adnan**
Photography by **Omar Mesrar**

Translated by
Hicham Rafik

1 I am not an expert when it comes to matters of sport, but, like any Moroccan, I am passionate about football and its news. And because passion is a part of sports, I found myself following the local team, al-Kawkab al-Marrakeshi. But I've fixed on Raja Club Athletic, in Casablanca, as the team I follow for its news and moments of joy. Fact is, I chose Raja not for its stars nor for its honors, but mainly because of its fans. These historic fans cover the stadium in art in a way that Raja never will.

The tifos of Raja's ultras roam Arabic websites, and everyone waits for them, such that they are received in all Arab countries, from the Atlantic Ocean to the Gulf. As for the chants of the Raja fans, even children in the streets and alleys of Casablanca have learned them by heart. Moreover, Raja fans remain the most concerned with national issues. It is a highly politicized audience. It's an audience that stands in solidarity with the Palestinian cause in an inauspicious time, when nationalism is falling. "Lahbiba ya Palestine," the famous chant that many musicians reworked and redistributed during their concerts, was even repeated at rallies in solidarity with Palestine—even in Mashreqi countries, where people long considered the Moroccan accent too hard to understand. As for Raja supporters' chants that stand in solidarity with the oppressed and marginalized people of Morocco, even teachers and doctors don't mind singing them during their protests. Moreover, Raja fans are authentic in a special way. Before the confinement, Raja fans left the stadium and headed for the home of a Raja fan who has cancer. Legions gathered before his window, where the Raja songs rang out for about an hour while the patient waved weakly in an emotional scene. Such fans are unparalleled throughout the Arab world. And for this, I adore Raja. First and foremost, because of those fans.

And when the Raja team qualified for the 2013 FIFA Club World Championship, which was held in Marrakesh, I went to watch the great game between Raja, which was the Arab and African football representative, and Bayern Munich, the winner of the UEFA Champions League. But instead of watching the game, I found myself spending all my time following the Raja fans, who were continuously doing loud waves and enthusiastic chants. Only after the game came to an end did I discover that I had attended an important match, yet without succeeding in watching it. Fortunately, there are a few channels that rebroadcast the games. When I was back home, I searched among these channels and watched the game, from which Raja fans had stolen my attention.

© Omar Mesrar

Every once in a while, I surprise my friends with articles or at least blogs that discuss matters of national football. But as much as these articles make some people happy, others grow resentful. The idea, they say, is that football is the opium of the Arab nations, and that we, as writers and operators in the fields of culture, have to be cautious and suspicious of it. Well yes, it's an opium, but where is the problem? I think when Karl Marx wrote that religion was the opium of the masses, he didn't mean it was a drug, but a balm. Opium in Marx's time was a painkiller. Like football, it can ease the wounds of nations, poor and rich, and provide them with a reason for entertainment and relief. And who says that being affiliated with the fields of literature and culture puts one outside the circle of football aficionados, as if this is not a noble sport, but rather a mean activity strictly for the masses? This is wrong. Literature has a special relationship with sport, and especially with football. Not just because many novelists worked this sport into their stories and novels, as I personally did in my novel *Hot Maroc*, but also because many writers were athletes, and especially football players.

For instance, Albert Camus, winner of a Nobel Prize, was goalkeeper for the University of Algiers team in the 1930 season.

The Russian novelist Vladimir Nabokov was also a goalkeeper, as was the Russian poet Yevtushenko. And in Morocco, we have many well-known literary names with roots in the world of football, such as the poet Ahmed Sabri, who was a football player and then a coach. In Marrakesh too, the poet Jamal Amach and the novelist Abd Elaziz Ait Bensaleh were football players before they devoted themselves to literature, which happened after they had retired from playing football; the former was best known as a poet and the latter as a novelist. The author of the novel *Moroccans*, Abdelkarim Jouaiti, was a great fan of football, and he served as president of the club Raja Beni Mellal. Football played a strong and comic role in his novel *Platoon of Ruin*, the first Moroccan novel to be longlisted for the International Prize for Arabic Fiction.

Personally, to this day, I still play football, although I am careful not to be played by it, especially as I have witnessed how football is used to manipulate crowds. In the early 80s, when I was an adolescent, the city's first team, al-Kawkab al-Marrakeshi, was in the second national division. But right after the 1984 popular uprising—in which students from Marrakesh were deeply involved, and which was violently suppressed by the authorities—the latter noticed the need to distract the city's youngsters with something that would make them numb and distract them from politics and protests. It was agreed that al-Kawkab al-Marrakeshi was the solution. Mohamed Mediouri, a loyal son of the city, was serving as the Head of Personal Security for the late King Hassan II. The king ordered him to manage the team, and so it was. Al-Kawkab al-Marrakeshi climbed to the first national division, and all the city's events were built around it. Local authorities, as well as regional economic institutions, dedicated themselves to providing reasons to support the team, trying to get closer to the new president. And so al-Kawkab al-Marrakeshi became an unstoppable team, especially at home. We used to go to the Harthy Stadium in Marrakech, already reassured of the score, even if the other team was first to score a goal. We knew the referee would give us a penalty just at the right time, even if it was imaginary, just to please the personal guard of the King and to send their compliments. That was how al-Kawkab al-Marrakeshi became the champion, with some honors that were deserved, and some that were achieved by other means. Getting young people to follow the team multiplied its fans. Perhaps al-Kawkab al-Marrakeshi was one of the reasons for the social stability of the Almoravid capital from the late 1980s to mid-1990s.

3 Once, in Berlin, I was on a panel with the great Algerian novelist Rachid Boujedra, sponsored by the Heinrich Böll Foundation. The Germans who attended the seminar were expecting that a face-to-face meeting of a Moroccan and Algerian would be heated, and, more than that, that we would start judging and blaming each other's politics. Political tensions between Rabat and El Mouradia Palace were particularly high at the time. But the author of *Penalty Shootout* set politics and literature aside and surprised the Germans with an amusing conversation about the relationship between Morocco, Algeria, and Germany, starting with football and the contests in our respective home countries. All of us remembered the historic win against Germany in the 1982 World Cup that was hosted in Spain. Algeria was about to move on to the second round—and they would have, if Germany and Austria hadn't plotted against them, agreeing to a draw and playing a game that lacked sportsmanship, which meant Algeria lost the chance to move to the second round. This was the scandal that led to FIFA's adoption of a new system, through which the last round of the group stage was played on the same day and time, avoiding any future complicity between the participating teams. And thus a spot in the second round was postponed, for Arab and African football, to the 1986 World Cup in Mexico. There, the Moroccan team was the first Arab and African team to reach the round of 16, before we got knocked out by the Germans. May God forgive them. The Germans are on the lookout for the Maghrebi teams. In fact, our national team held out against the German machines until the last two minutes, before Matthäus scored a goal. During that meeting, shootouts continued to flow, but all of them were licit. Most of them hit the goal and deserved an ovation.

But, what about when the poet applauds the football player? As if it needs a poet like Mahmoud Darwish to publicly declare his adoration for football. Without any hesitation, the poet of the Palestinian cause wrote a beautiful and fine work that was like love poetry for the Argentinian star Diego Maradona: "Strong as a bull. Fast as a missile. He enters the stadium as if entering a church. He sifts through the defense and scores. The star of his time. Doctors won't find blood in his veins. They will find rocket fuel."

Ronaldo and Messi have the right to consider themselves unlucky: They missed being watched by that great lover of the game, Mahmoud Darwish.

Join

Us!

Advertise in ArabLit Quarterly to reach an audience that cares
about the written word ... and support
an award-winning independent magazine with a passion for
translation and Arabic literature.

ARABLIT QUARTERLY

Contact us at info@arablit.org.

Excerpt

What looks like somewhere in Morocco is actually in Cheshire Oaks Way, Ellesmere Port, UK
© Humphrey Muleba; Unsplash

Hot Maroc

By **Yassin Adnan**

Don Quixote? Did you say Don Quixote?

Don Quixote is tall, Qamar Eddine. True, he was thin, but he was slim and tall. Yazid is short and pudgy. How could he remind you of him? But Qamar Eddine wasn't thinking about height or girth. Rather, what he was thinking about was Sancho. Ever since a follower of Yazid's started to stick to him like a shadow, this nickname had stuck and he began to promote it in the cybercafe, when Yazid wasn't there, of course (even though Rabih, who was of medium build, didn't look like Sancho at all). He could be sure no one in the cybercafe had read Cervantes. But Fadoua, Samira, and Salim had watched the dubbed cartoon series *Don Quixote de la Mancha* and they knew what Qamar Eddine was talking about.

Translated by
Alexander Elinson

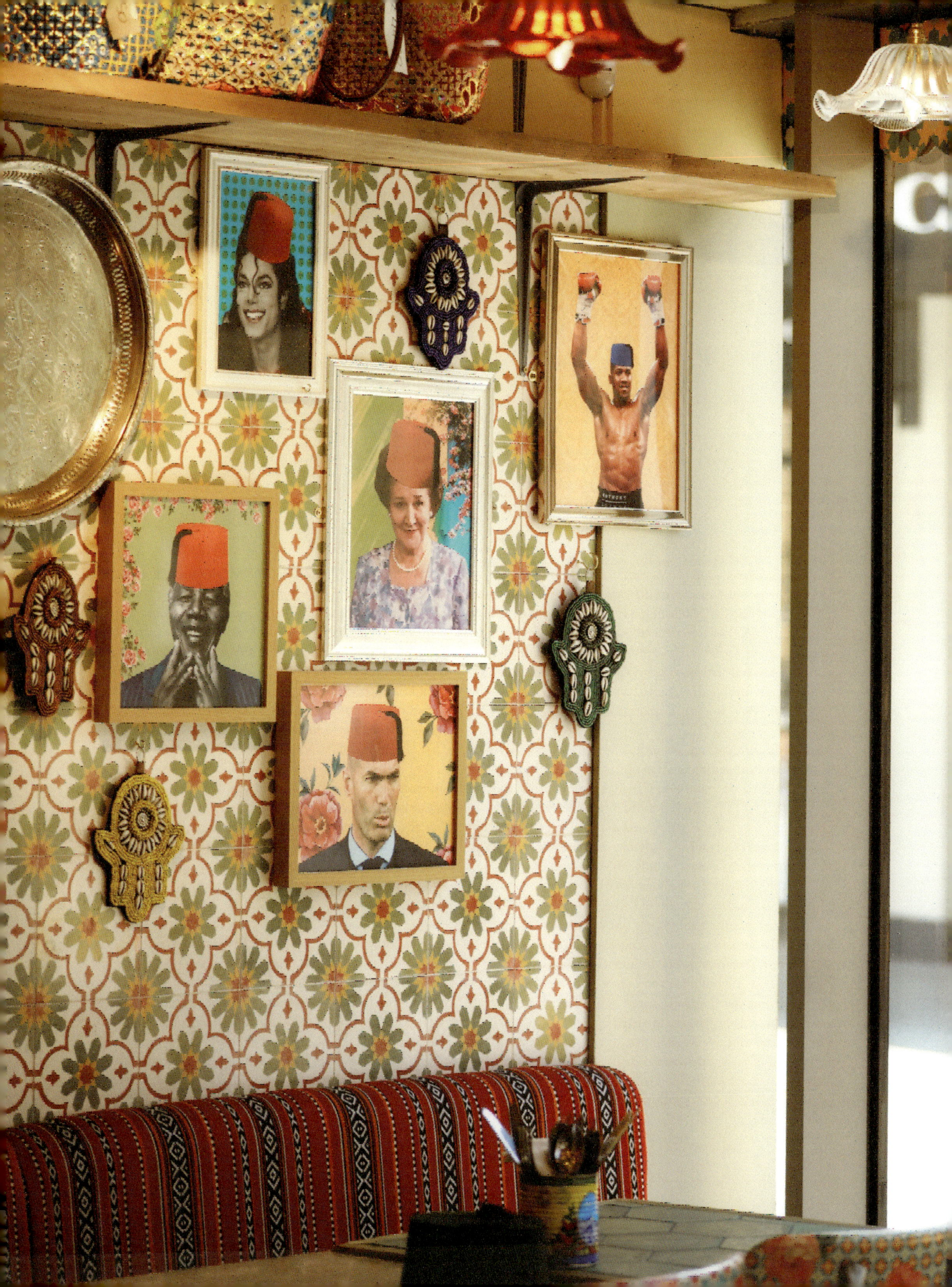

But where did the Don Quixote of Dakhla Avenue find this obedient follower who didn't mind waiting hours for Yazid outside the cybercafe door? A wait that wasn't without its uses. Because after less than a month, Yazid arranged a small job for him next door as a cigarette vendor and bicycle guardian. There, between a small line of randomly planted orange trees to the right of Café Milano, Yazid improvised a parking area for bicycles and mopeds. Rabih didn't work himself to death morning and evening. Rather, only when there was a soccer match. And because the soccer schedules had started to become more noticeably frequent, he had come to work guarding the bicycles more and more. Basically, whenever soccer fans filled the cafés. Especially lovers of the Spanish league. Everyone followed La Liga in the cafés of Dakhla Avenue. All the cafés started to show the matches live, and also made a rebroadcast available the morning after. Years ago, each café on Dakhla Avenue had customers of specific sorts. The Hanafi Café, for example, was for building contractors and their customers. The Taysir Café was specifically for used-car salesmen. Morning and evening, vehicles of different models were lined up out front. Some vendors practically entered the café by car so that dealers and potential customers could inspect them without leaving their chairs. The Hope Café was the official haunt for youth associations; young writers and playwrights who saw themselves as the neighborhood's vanguard. And since there was no youth club in Massira, their scholarly group met every day at the Hope Café. When they established their Masar theater troupe and a choir dedicated to politically engaged songs, the café became the de facto headquarters for these two new associations. It was natural, then, that this café in particular would face periodic police raids, resulting in its customers—who were steadfast artists—being taken down to the Massira police station on drug charges. The Farid Atrache Café, which is only three doors down from the Hope Café, was considered the permanent headquarters of the most famous drug dealer in the neighborhood, Omar Bouri. That's why this café received regular visits from police officers and detectives. Not to make raids and arrests, but rather, to get whatever the mood required from Omar Bouri, all at good prices. After midnight, some of the neighborhood boys would sneak to the upper level of the café, where they would always show porn flicks to a rapt audience. Café Milano was the favored space for teachers from Massira High School, as well as an elite group of employees who could be described as "honorable," but in recent years, when Talios made it his headquarters as his star was rising, so-called business and people wanting to emigrate in intricate ways crawled to him and transformed Café Milano into a nest of scum, as Asmae described it. But now, all the cafés of Dakhla Avenue had come to resemble one another after having been transformed into bleacher seats for soccer games. A huge stadium that extended the length of the street. The owner of Café Milano is a Real Madrid fan, so he forces the waiter who helps Asmae in the evenings to wear the Real jersey while he's working. Despite that, the majority of Café Milano's customers are Barcelona fans. There is a minimal level of democracy at Café Milano, and there's generally space for the two audiences to interact. The situation is more extreme in the Farid Atrache Café. Omar Bouri, who visited Barcelona in the mid-1980s and who claims that the love of his life was from Barcelona, absolutely forbids Real fans to enter the café. Omar Bouri is the café's mayor, the one who gets the final word there. Therefore, even the owner of the Farid Atrache Café has to embrace the Catalan creed, whether he likes it or not.

With odd regularity, Rabih would stand in front of Café Milano, ready to offer the right type of cigarette to whoever asked for it, then he'd go back to his post, fulfilling both of his tasks. One eye on the bicycles and the other on the café's clientele. Clouds of smoke float above the heads of those watching as they shout and yell insults. The customers smoke, provide commentary, and bad-mouth the players. They're all soccer experts. High-level specialists. They explained the strategies while smoking, coughing, and spitting. They all knew more than the coaches, they adjudicated the game better than the referees, and they criticized the players and told them—albeit too late—the shortest route to the goal and the best ways to exploit missed opportunities.

True, most of them don't play sports at all, neither soccer nor basketball, nor do they even walk much. But their sporting instincts are extremely well-honed. Some of them can give you a perfect report of the Spanish championships from the last five years that includes all the details on how the best and worst teams did. They compete with one another in memorizing the millions of euros that contracts are worth and that result in players moving around the league, all while they rifle through their empty pockets searching for enough change for a measly cup of coffee. Virtual athletes, following only on-screen and as spectators. But frankly, not to unfairly disparage the soccer fans, *all* Moroccans live their lives on-screen. The television screen or the computer screen. They know all countries through tourism and travel shows. All nationalities by way of Facebook. They're addicted to political television shows and they accept heated political debate on Facebook, yet they are withdrawn from the political party life of their country. The majority of them are covetous of their political purity, like wholesome, untouched virgins. Therefore, it's rare for them to cast their votes in elections.

Life is elsewhere. It's there. On-screen. Gooooooal! The match is intense and, as usual, the commentator makes you see what isn't there, deftly rhyming: "Fire, fire, fire, it's down to the wire . . . Messi is a sly one. The damage is done . . . Here's Messi, folks . . . the one with the diamond foot . . . with the header in goal . . . Finally, Messi makes joy erupt . . . and wins the cup!"

But Rabih wasn't interested in the cup or the championship. He's here to work. He left his Berber village of Tadarte, which sits on top of Mount Tichka, in search of work in Marrakech. He stayed with his relative, a doorman in the building where Moulay Ahmed Malkha lived, and that's where he met his son, Yazid, and began to work for him. He's happy with his new situation, and it doesn't bother him at all to play the role of Sancho.

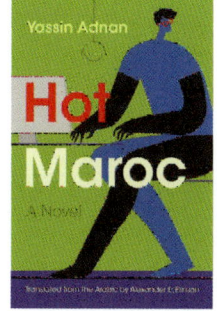

This excerpt, Chapter 60 of **Hot Maroc**, appears with permission from Syracuse University Press.

Dictionary

Final Whistle

By **Hassân Al Mohtasib**

I remember that boring hot day during the school summer vacation in Jordan. I remember my fervent laments that there was *nothing* on TV and that the books in my father's library were all "finished." I had read stacks and stacks of books. But that day, one of the magazines my father subscribed to, from the Arab States Broadcasting Union, came to my rescue. In such magazines, they covered everything about the profession of broadcasters, journalists or radio reporters. In this issue, there was an article about the standardization of the Arabic term for offside.

In the Maghreb, the word شرود was common: a beautiful word that precisely describes visually how a subject leaves his "flock" and swarms out. The Mashreqi word, which was more familiar to me, was تسلل, which roughly means infiltration by stealth. The evocation of this vocabulary struck my boredom away.

In general, football is an arena for nonviolent acts of war. *Battles* to be won. *Campaigns* to be plotted. *Strategies* are set and *tactics* are to be followed. Players *fight* to win and *spoils of war* are counted in points. Yet the offside has a semantic system all its own. Maybe that's why offside is so special; frustrating and yet also so exciting.

It is the tip-of-the-fingers energy, not that of a firm fist. Criminal not military energy that's sparked. It is the act of an individual that forces the game from its military macro-level to its micro-level of individual attack. Positions at the time of the "crime" are registered and analyzed *forensically*. Lines are drawn on the pitch, if only virtually. They encircle not only the victim, but also the perpetrator.

Amongst the guild of crime writers, it is said that the reader must not know more than the detective. This is a built-in handicap for the reader, wherein the tension is created by refusing to allow the reader a bird's eye view, but rather to build tension by placing an obstacle in front of one's vision. On the pitch, we are all the reader. There, the detective doesn't bite on a pipe but a whistle, and the magnifying glass is called VAR. It is the power of the width of a blade of grass that may be decisive for the outcome of a battle.

LIV 1-1 WOL
48:43 +3'

CHECKING GOAL - POSSIBLE OFFSIDE

Contributors

Farid Abdel Azim is an Egyptian novelist born in 1983. He has published a number of short stories in newspapers and on online platforms. He won a prize for his short story collection in 2016. In 2018 he participated in the project to support writing talent in the MENA region (the Cairo Short Stories project), organized by the Goethe-institut in collaboration with the German KFW Development Bank.

Yassin Adnan (born in Safi in 1970) has lived in Marrakech since he was a young child. Since 2006, he has researched and hosted his weekly cultural TV program *Macharef* (Thresholds) on Morocco's Channel One. Since 2019 he has hosted a new cultural TV program *Bayt Yassin* (Yassin's Home). He is the author of four published collections of poetry in Arabic and also has three short story collections. He co-wrote *Marrakech: Open Secrets* (2008) with Saad Sarhane. He is the editor of *The Moroccan Scheherazade: Testimonies and Studies of Fatima Mernissi* (2016), *Marrakech: evanescent places* (2018), and *Marrakech Noir* (2018). His first novel, *Hot Maroc* (2016), was nominated for The International Prize for Arabic Fiction in 2017. The English translation of *Hot Maroc* (translated by Alexander Elinson) appeared in August 2021, published by Syracuse University Press.

Hatem Alzahrani is an awarded poet, critic, translator, and an academic specializing in Middle Eastern cultures and Arabic literature. He has an MA degree in Near Eastern Studies from Yale University (2014) and Ph.D. from Georgetown University (2019). He has published two collections of poetry: *The Letter Yā' Is Mine* (2009) and *Celebrating the Dual at Yale* (2019).

Daniel Behar is a postdoctoral fellow for Jewish Studies and Middle Eastern Studies at Dartmouth College. He works on modern and contemporary poetry from Syria. His poetry translations from Arabic have appeared in several literary journals.

Najwa Bin Shatwan is a Libyan academic and novelist, the first Libyan to ever be shortlisted for the International Prize of Arabic Fiction (in 2017). She has authored four novels, in addition to several collections of short stories, plays and contributions to anthologies. She was chosen as one of the thirty-nine best Arab authors under the age of forty by Hay Festival's Beirut 39 project (2009). In 2018, she was chosen from hundreds of Arab writers for the 2018 Banipal Writing Fellowship Residency at the University of Durham.

Khadidja Bouchellia is a PhD student and a teaching assistant at the University of Arkansas.

Huda al-Daghfaq is a Saudi poet and journalist with several published poetry anthologies to her name. She writes for cultural and literary magazines, and has undertaken research in the fields of social studies, philosophy, and women's rights. Her work has been translated into English, French, Italian and Spanish.

Luqman Derky (1966-) is a Kurdish-Syrian poet, actor, dissident blogger and cultural organizer from the town of Darbasiya on the Turkish-Syrian border. He now lives between France and Germany. Derky was a member of the University of Aleppo Literary Forum. A volume of his collected poems appeared in 2006 with Dar Nainawa press.

Alexander E. Elinson is head of the Arabic Program at Hunter College of the City University of New. He is the author of *Looking Back: The Poetics of Loss and Nostalgia in Medieval Arabic and Hebrew Literature* (2009). He has also published translations of Moroccan poetry and fiction into English that include works by Allal Bourqia, Adil Latefi, Ahmed Lemsyeh, Driss Mesnaoui, and two novels by Youssef Fadel: *A Beautiful White Cat Walks with Me* (2016) and *A Shimmering Red Fish Swims with Me* (2019), which was shortlisted for the 2020 Saif Ghobash Banipal Prize for Arabic literary translation. He is currently translating Khadija Marouazi's *Biography of Ash* which will be published in 2022.

Zeena Faulk is the principal translator of the known 78 Shalash blog posts that appeared on kitabat. She is an Iraqi-American literary translator and a PhD candidate in Translation Studies at the University of Warwick. She was recently shortlisted for the Gabo Prize in Literary Translation and her translated works have appeared in *Banipal, ArabLit Quarterly, Lunch Ticket, Passa Porta,* among others. Her previous work includes managing editor and translator positions with the Mayo Clinic and Cleveland Clinic. She also works as an on-site interpreter for criminal courts and medical clinics throughout the United States.

Moneera Al-Ghadeer was a Visiting Professor of comparative literature in the Department of Middle Eastern, South Asian, and African Studies at Columbia University and was a Shawwaf Visiting Professor at Harvard University. She was a tenured Professor at the University of Wisconsin-Madison and received her Ph.D. from the University of California, Berkeley. She has published *Desert Voices: Bedouin Women's Poetry in Saudi Arabia* (I.B. Tauris, 2009) as well as many articles, book chapters, and translations.

Muhammad El-Hajj is a writer based in Cairo. He is the author of *Nobody Mourns the City's Cats* (2018), which won the 2019 Sawiris Cultural Award, and the critically acclaimed 2013 film *Villa 69*. His second collection of short fiction, *Two Stories About Masculinity*, from which this excerpt is taken, is set to be released later this year.

Ameer Hamad was born in Jerusalem in 1992. He holds a degree in computer science from Birzeit University. In 2019, he was awarded the Al-Qattan prize in two categories for his first two books: *Gigi and Ali's Rabbit*, a collection of short stories, and *I Searched for Their Keys in the Locks*, a collection of poetry (both forthcoming this year from Al Ahlia).

Yasmeen Hanoosh is a fiction writer, literary translator, and professor at Portland State University, where she directs the Arabic program and teaches courses in Arabic language and literature. She has published a short story collection, *Ardh al-Khayrat al-Mal'unah* (The Land of Cursed Riches, Al-Ahali Press, 2021). Her second collection, *Atfal al-Jannah al-Mankubah* (Children of Afflicted Paradise) has been translated and excerpted in multiple languages, including English, Spanish, and Italian. Her translations of Arabic fiction have appeared in various literary journals and publications. Her translation of *Closing His Eyes* (Abbas) received an NEA translation fellowship in 2010, and her translation of *Scattered Crumbs* (al-Ramli) won the Arkansas Arabic Translation Prize in 2002.

Mina Ibrahim is completing his PhD in Cultural Studies at the University of Gießen (JLU) and is a lecturer at the University of Marburg. He has been a doctoral fellow at GCSC and SFB/TRR 138 in Germany, OIB in Lebanon, and CEDEJ in Egypt. He is also the project coordinator of the MENA Prison Forum (MPF) and the cofounder of Shubra's Archive for Research and Development (SARD). His publications include articles with Social Compass, Endowment Studies, and Middle East Topics and Arguments, and book chapters with Palgrave Macmillan and Vanderbilt University Press (forthcoming 2021 & 2022 respectively).

Omar Ibrahim is an Egyptian literary translator, poet and essayist. He has four published translations and a poetry collection. Among his translations are the Arabic translation of H.P. Lovecraft's *The Whisperer in Darkness* published in 2020 by Dar Dawen, and David Stuart Davies' *The Further Adventures of Sherlock Holmes: The Scroll of the Dead* published by Kayan for Publishing and Distribution.

Becki Maddock is a Research Analyst and Translator based in London, UK. She has a BA (Hons) in Arabic & Spanish from Exeter University and an MA in Near & Middle East Studies from SOAS, University of London. Becki is a regular contributor to *Banipal* Magazine of Modern Arab Literature and runs the Banipal Book Club.

Hajar Mahfoodh is currently pursuing her Ph.D. in Literature at the University of Surrey, where she is working on exile and home in modern Arab poetry. Hajar is mainly interested in culture and preserving intangible culture and heritage. She is also interested in modern literature, creative writing, and postcolonial theory. Her passionate relationship with arts and poetry is expressed through her experimental poetry in both visual and written forms. Twitter: @HajarAlMahfoodh Insta: @ha_almahfoodh

Mahmoud Mostafa is an Egyptian journalist and translator based in the US. His work has been featured in *Jadaliyya*, *Almanassa*, and *Daily News Egypt* among others. He is passionate about football, cultural heritage, oral history, authors photographed next to their cats, and aubergine-based recipes, along with other equally important topics.

Hicham Rafik is a young enthusiast, English teacher, chorister, translator and interpreter. He graduated from Mohammed V University with a focus on Cultural Translation.

Leonie Rau is a Master's student in Islamic and Middle Eastern Studies at the University of Tübingen, Germany, and hopes to pursue a PhD after her graduation. She is an aspiring literary translator with a particular interest in Maghrebi literature. She also writes and edits for ArabLit and *ArabLit Quarterly* and can be found on Twitter @Leonie_Rau_.

S

Iraqi Shalash is the pseudonym for an Iraqi blogger who posted mostly satirical blogs in a hybrid Arabic form between 2005 and 2006. The Iraqi Shalash blogs first emerged on the popular blogosphere *kitabat* — criticizing key social issues, mocking the multiple political and religious groups in Iraq, and exposing the corrupt government in unique ways that struck a chord with the average Iraqis. Several Iraqi journalists and writers claimed the identity of this blogger, but these Shalash wannabees failed to prove it. For unknown reasons, Shalash stopped posting new blogs in 2006, which pushed the readers to think that the blogger was ambushed and killed by the groups mocked in the blogs. To this day, the real identity of this blogger remains a mystery.

Adania Shibli (1974, Palestine) has been writing novels, plays, short stories and narrative essays, which were published in various anthologies, art books, and literary and cultural magazines in different languages. She has twice been awarded with the Qattan Young Writer's Award-Palestine in 2001 for her novel *Masaas* (translated into English as *Touch*. Northampton: Clockroot), and in 2003 for her novel *Kulluna Ba'id bethat al Miqdar aan el-Hub* (translated into English as *We Are All Equally Far from Love*. Northampton: Clockroot). Her latest novel is *Tafsil Thanawi* (*Minor Detail*, Beirut: Al-Adab). Amongst her non-fiction books are, the art book *Dispositions* (Ramallah: Qattan), and an edited collection of essays *A Journey of Ideas Across: In Dialog with Edward Said*, (Berlin: HKW).

Lameen Souag grew up in America, Algeria, and the UK before becoming a researcher at the CNRS in France. His main focus is on the linguistic history of North and West Africa and what it can tell us about how languages change more generally. He has worked on documenting two minority languages of the Sahara, Korandje and Siwi, and on describing the grammar of Algerian Arabic. He enjoys swimming, ideally along a rocky shore, but hardly ever watches or plays football.

Y

Khalid Ahmed Youssef is a filmmaker, writer, and photographer. Born in Cairo. Baptized in Madrid. Living in Chicago.

Nariman Youssef is a Cairo-born, London-based semi-freelance literary translator. She holds a master's degree in translation studies from the University of Edinburgh, manages a small translation team at the British Library, and curates translation workshops with Shadow Heroes. Her literary translations include Inaam Kachachi's *The American Granddaughter* (Interlink Books, 2021), Donia Kamal's *Cigarette Number Seven* (American University in Cairo Press, 2018), and contributions in *Words Without Borders, The Common, Banipal*, and the poetry anthologies *Beirut39* (Bloodaxe, 2014) and *The Hundred Years' War* (Bloomsbury, 2010).

Z

Anam Zafar translates from Arabic and French into English so misrepresented communities can tell their own stories on their own terms. She was a 2020/21 mentee on the National Centre for Writing's Emerging Translators Mentorship scheme, and was a translator in residence at the Centre in May 2021. She also volunteers for World Kid Lit.

Yasmine Zohdi is a writer, editor and translator based in Cairo. She has an MFA in fiction from Sarah Lawrence College, New York, and is currently working on her first short story collection.

Printed in Great Britain
by Amazon